Better Homes and Gardens®

Best Barbecue Recipes

Our seal assures you that every recipe in *Best Barbecue Recipes*
has been tested in the Better Homes and Gardens® Test Kitchen.
This means that each recipe is practical and reliable,
and meets our high standards of taste appeal.

BETTER HOMES AND GARDENS® BOOKS
Editor: Gerald M. Knox
Art Director: Ernest Shelton
Managing Editor: David A. Kirchner
Editorial Project Managers: Liz Anderson, James D. Blume,
    Marsha Jahns

Department Head, Cook Books: Sharyl Heiken
Associate Department Heads: Sandra Granseth,
    Rosemary C. Hutchinson, Elizabeth Woolever
Senior Food Editors: Linda Henry, Marcia Stanley, Joyce Trollope
Associate Food Editors: Jennifer Darling, Heather M. Hephner,
    Mary Major, Shelli McConnell, Mary Jo Plutt
Test Kitchen: Director, Sharon Stilwell; Photo Studio Director,
    Janet Herwig; Home Economists: Kay Cargill, Marilyn Cornelius,
    Maryellyn Krantz, Lynelle Munn, Marge Steenson,
    Colleen Weeden

Associate Art Directors: Neoma Thomas, Linda Ford Vermie,
    Randall Yontz
Assistant Art Directors: Lynda Haupert, Harijs Priekulis, Tom Wegner
Graphic Designers: Mary Schlueter Bendgen, Mike Burns,
    Brian Wignall
Art Production: Director, John Berg; Associate, Joe Heuer;
    Office Manager, Michaela Lester

President, Book Group: Jeramy Lanigan
Vice President, Retail Marketing: Jamie L. Martin
Vice President, Administrative Services: Rick Rundall

BETTER HOMES AND GARDENS® MAGAZINE
President, Magazine Group: James A. Autry
Editorial Director: Doris Eby
Editorial Services Director: Duane L. Gregg
Food and Nutrition Editor: Nancy Byal

MEREDITH CORPORATION OFFICERS
Chairman of the Executive Committee: E. T. Meredith III
Chairman of the Board: Robert A. Burnett
President: Jack D. Rehm

BEST BARBECUE RECIPES
Editor: Marcia Stanley
Editorial Project Manager: James D. Blume
Graphic Designer: Tom Wegner
Electronic Text Processor: Paula Forest
Contributing Photographer: M. Jensen Photography, Inc.
Food Stylists: JoAnn Cherry, Suzanne Finley
Contributing Illustrator: Buck Jones

On the cover: *Apricot Ribs*
(see recipe, page 46)

Contents

4 Grilling Basics
General information to get you started barbecuing.

6 Steaks and Chops
Marinated, sauced, or stuffed meat grilled to perfection.

20 Sauces
Everything in barbecue sauce, from fiery hot to super fast.

24 Burgers and More
All kinds of burgers cooked on the grill.

36 Relishes
Sandwich toppings to fit any fancy.

38 Ribs and More Ribs
Pork and beef ribs dripping with sauce.

48 Poultry Pieces
A variety of turkey and chicken pieces perfect for the whole family.

58 Robust Roasts and Birds
Juicy roasts and whole birds slowly grilled over indirect heat.

68 Kabob Cookery
A sizzling assortment of skewered meats and vegetables.

72 Baskets of Fish and Shellfish
Grill baskets full of seafood favorites.

76 Grilling Charts
Timings for commonly grilled meats.

79 Index

Grilling Basics

Ahh! Summertime! It's the time for getting together with friends, boating on the lake, and, of course, cooking dinner on the backyard grill. And to help you enjoy summer to its fullest, we've gathered the best

of barbecue recipes—recipes for sizzling steaks, ribs dripping with sauce, old-fashioned and newfangled burgers, juicy grilled chicken, and much more.

But before you begin, take a look at the information about grilling fundamentals on these two pages. Spend just a few minutes now looking over these tips and you'll have a successful backyard barbecue every time.

Selecting a grill
Choose the grill that best fits your needs.

Braziers are relatively inexpensive uncovered grills with shallow fireboxes that are designed for direct cooking. They have three or four legs and range from the simplest grills to elaborate units with half hoods, rotisseries, and air vents.

Hibachis are small, portable grills that are great for directly grilling small foods. Most come equipped with adjustable grill racks, air vents, and

briquette racks to let ashes sift to the bottom.

Kettle or *wagon* grills are large and resemble kettles or covered wagons. Although these grills differ from brand to brand, they all feature air vents in their bottoms and grill hoods or full domed lids to control ventilation. Both types can be used for direct or indirect cooking. And both are available with charcoal, gas, or electric cooking units. Check your owner's manual for operating instructions for gas or electric grills.

Preparing the firebox
Cooking with charcoal grills requires a few more steps than with gas or electric grills. Many manufacturers recommend that you line the firebox with heavy-duty foil and add an inch of pea gravel or coarse grit. After you've used the grill a dozen times, change the foil and wash and dry the gravel or grit bedding.

Spreading the charcoal briquettes
Estimate the number of charcoal briquettes needed by spreading them out into a single layer, extending them about an inch beyond the size of the food to be cooked. On windy or humid days, or for longer-cooking foods, you may need slightly more charcoal.

Starting the grill
Pile the briquettes into a pyramid or mound in the center of the firebox. Drizzle liquid lighter or jelly fire starter over the entire charcoal surface. Wait for one minute, then ignite with a match. (Never use gasoline or kerosene to start charcoal.)

For faster starting, use an electric fire starter according to the manufacturer's directions. Charcoal is ready for grilling when it's glowing or gray and has no black showing. This usually takes 20 to 30 minutes.

Arranging the coals
Once the coals are ready, spread them out according to the appropriate directions below.

Direct cooking: Use long-handled tongs to spread the hot coals into a single layer. For more even heat and fewer flare-ups, arrange the coals a half inch apart.

Indirect cooking: Use a disposable foil drip pan or make your own using heavy-duty foil shaped into a shallow pan shape. Place the pan in the center of the firebox, then use long-handled tongs to arrange the coals in a circle around the pan.

Judging the heat of the coals
Determine the temperature of the coals by holding your hand, palm side down, above the coals at the height your food will be cooked. Then start counting the seconds, "one thousand one, one thousand two." If you need to withdraw your hand after two seconds, the coals are *hot;* after three seconds, they're *medium-hot;* after four seconds, they're *medium;* after five seconds, they're *medium-slow;* and after six seconds, they're *slow.* If you need to adjust the temperature of the coals, check the tip on page 73.

For indirect cooking, *hot* coals provide *medium-hot* heat over the drip pan. *Medium-hot* coals provide *medium* heat, *medium* coals provide *medium-slow heat,* and so on.

Controlling the fire
Fat and meat juices dripping onto hot coals can cause flare-ups. These sudden blazes will burn your meat, resulting in a charred flavor. You can reduce flare-ups by raising the grill rack, covering the grill, spacing the hot coals farther apart, or removing a few coals. As a last resort, remove the food from the grill and

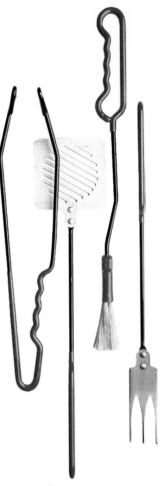

mist the fire with a pump-spray bottle filled with water. When the flare-up has died, return the food to the grill.

Selecting utensils
To protect yourself from the heat of the grill, long-handled utensils are a must. You'll need long-handled tongs to arrange hot coals and turn steaks. You can use a long-handled spatula to turn burgers. And you'll find a long-handled fork is handy when you're arranging foods on the grill.

Washing the grill
Clean your grill rack immediately after cooking. Just soak it in a sinkful of hot, sudsy water, then wipe off the grime. Use a stiff grill brush for any stubborn spots. If your grill rack is too large to fit into the sink, cover both sides of the rack with wet paper towels or newspapers and let the rack stand for an hour or so. Remove the paper and wash off the food. Don't use abrasive cleaning products on your grill rack without checking its manufacturer's directions.

Onion- and Spinach-Stuffed Steaks

2 beef top loin steaks, cut 1 inch thick	● Cut a pocket in each steak by cutting from the fat side almost to the bone.

½ cup chopped onion 2 cloves garlic, minced 1 tablespoon margarine *or* butter ½ of a 10-ounce package frozen chopped spinach, thawed and well drained ½ teaspoon dried marjoram, crushed ¼ teaspoon salt ⅛ teaspoon pepper	● For stuffing, in a saucepan cook the chopped onion and minced garlic in margarine or butter till tender. Stir in the drained spinach, dried marjoram, salt, and pepper. Spoon stuffing into the steak pockets. Fasten pockets with wooden toothpicks.

● Grill steaks on an uncovered grill directly over *medium-hot* coals to desired doneness, turning once. (Allow 8 to 12 minutes for rare, 12 to 15 minutes for medium, and 16 to 20 minutes for well-done.) Makes 2 servings.

Nutrition information per serving: 362 calories, 41 g protein, 7 g carbohydrate, 19 g fat, 101 mg cholesterol, 477 mg sodium, 838 mg potassium.

Serving Suggestion:
Parmesan Tomato Slices
Tear off two 9x18-inch pieces of heavy-duty foil. Fold each in half to make a square. Slice 1 large *tomato* into ½-inch-thick slices. Top *each* foil square with *half* of the tomato slices. Sprinkle ⅛ teaspoon crushed *dried basil* over the tomato. Sprinkle with 2 tablespoons grated *Parmesan cheese.* Wrap foil around tomatoes, leaving space for steam to build. Place on grill rack beside steaks. Grill over coals for 6 to 8 minutes or till heated through.

Steak Doneness

Think it's impossible to cook steaks just right? Don't be intimidated. Just cut into your steaks and compare them to the photos at left.

Rare steak is red in the center, pink on the edges.

Medium steak still has a little pink in the center, but the edges are gray or brown.

Well-done steak is completely cooked all the way through with no pink remaining.

If you prefer medium-rare doneness, cook your steaks till they look halfway between rare and medium. For medium-well doneness, cook till the steaks appear halfway between medium and well-done.

Mushroom-Horseradish-Stuffed Steaks

4	**10-ounce beef top loin steaks, cut 1 inch thick**
1½	**cups sliced fresh mushrooms**
1	**medium onion, chopped**
2	**cloves garlic, minced**
1	**tablespoon margarine *or* butter**
2	**tablespoons prepared horseradish**

● Cut a pocket in each steak by cutting from the fat side almost to the bone. For stuffing, in a saucepan cook mushrooms, onion, and garlic in the margarine or butter till tender. Stir in horseradish, ¼ teaspoon *salt,* and ⅛ teaspoon *pepper.* Spoon the stuffing into the steak pockets. Fasten pockets with wooden toothpicks.

If you're a horseradish fan, these steaks are for you. The horseradish lovers on our taste panel raved about the stuffing's heat and zip.

2	**tablespoons margarine *or* butter, melted**
1	**tablespoon Worcestershire sauce**

● Combine margarine or butter and Worcestershire. Grill steaks on an uncovered grill directly over *medium-hot* coals to desired doneness, turning once and brushing with margarine mixture. (Allow 8 to 12 minutes for rare, 12 to 15 minutes for medium, and 16 to 20 minutes for well-done.) Serves 4.

Nutrition information per serving: 372 calories, 39 g protein, 5 g carbohydrate, 21 g fat, 101 mg cholesterol, 374 mg sodium, 688 mg potassium.

Chili-Oriental-Style Flank Steak

3	**tablespoons soy sauce**
2	**tablespoons dry sherry**
1	**tablespoon cooking oil**
2	**teaspoons chili powder**
2	**cloves garlic, minced**
½	**teaspoon ground ginger**
1	**1- to 1½-pound beef flank steak**

● Combine soy, sherry, oil, chili powder, garlic, ginger, and 2 tablespoons *water.* Score steak at 1-inch intervals in a diamond pattern on both sides. Place in a plastic bag set into a shallow dish. Pour marinade over steak. Close bag. Marinate in the refrigerator for 6 to 24 hours, turning occasionally.

It's a cultural exchange! The chili powder from Mexico and soy sauce from the Orient combine for a great-flavored marinade.

● Drain steak, reserving marinade. Grill on an uncovered grill directly over *medium* coals for 12 to 14 minutes or till medium-rare, turning once and brushing frequently with reserved marinade. To serve, slice the meat diagonally across the grain into very thin slices. Makes 4 servings.

Nutrition information per serving: 216 calories, 21 g protein, 1 g carbohydrate, 13 g fat, 58 mg cholesterol, 265 mg sodium, 358 mg potassium.

Cream-Sauced Steaks

| 3 | beef T-bone steaks, cut 1 inch thick |

● Grill steaks on an uncovered grill directly over *medium-hot* coals to desired doneness, turning once. (Allow 8 to 12 minutes for rare, 12 to 15 minutes for medium, and 16 to 20 minutes for well-done.) Cover; keep warm while preparing sauce.

For most people, half of a steak is plenty to eat. But if your family or guests are really hungry, you might want to serve only three with this recipe.

¾	cup sliced fresh mushrooms
⅓	cup sliced green onion
1	clove garlic, minced
2	tablespoons margarine *or* butter
2	teaspoons all-purpose flour
⅛	teaspoon salt
¾	cup light cream
3	tablespoons dry sherry

● For sauce, in a saucepan cook sliced mushrooms, green onion, and garlic in margarine or butter till tender. Stir in flour and salt. Stir in light cream. Cook and stir till mixture is slightly thickened and bubbly. Stir in sherry. Cook and stir for 1 minute more. Serve with steaks. Makes 3 to 6 servings.

Nutrition information per serving: 563 calories, 50 g protein, 7 g carbohydrate, 35 g fat, 165 mg cholesterol, 316 mg sodium, 828 mg potassium.

Bacon-Wrapped Tenderloins

4 slices bacon
2 beef tenderloin steaks, cut 1½ inches thick (about 1 pound total)

● In a skillet cook bacon till almost done but not crisp. Drain off fat. Pat bacon with paper towels to remove excess fat. Wrap bacon around steaks, securing with wooden toothpicks (see photo, right). Grill steaks on an uncovered grill directly over *medium-hot* coals to desired doneness, turning once. (Allow 14 to 18 minutes for rare, 18 to 22 minutes for medium, and 24 to 28 minutes for well-done.)

¼ pound fresh mushrooms, halved (1½ cups)
¼ cup chopped onion
½ teaspoon fines herbes
2 tablespoons margarine *or* butter

● Meanwhile, in a medium skillet cook the mushrooms, onion, and fines herbes in margarine or butter till mushrooms are tender. Remove from heat.

1 tablespoon dry sherry
2 teaspoons lime juice *or* lemon juice
⅛ teaspoon garlic salt

● Stir the sherry, lime juice or lemon juice, and garlic salt into the mushroom mixture. Serve over the grilled steaks. Makes 2 servings.

Nutrition information per serving: 453 calories, 35 g protein, 5 g carbohydrate, 31 g fat, 104 mg cholesterol, 554 mg sodium, 749 mg potassium.

Wrap two slices of bacon around the outside edge of each tenderloin steak. Secure the bacon to the steaks with wooden toothpicks.

Make the restaurant classic, filet mignon, right on your own grill. We topped our meat with sautéed mushrooms, but you can add a topping of your choice. Or just enjoy the grilled steaks plain.

Calorie-Trimmed Flank Steak

1 1¼- to 1½-pound beef flank steak	● Score steak on both sides (see tip, right), if necessary. Place steak in a plastic bag set into a shallow dish.	**Some grocery stores sell flank steak already scored. If your store doesn't, do the scoring yourself. Use a sharp knife to make shallow cuts at 1-inch intervals in a diamond pattern on the surface of the meat. Scoring shortens the meat fibers, making them more tender. It also allows more marinade to soak in.**
½ cup reduced-calorie clear Italian salad dressing ⅓ cup soy sauce ⅓ cup dry red *or* white wine 3 tablespoons sliced green onion 3 lemon slices, cut ⅛ inch thick ½ teaspoon dry mustard ¼ teaspoon lemon-pepper seasoning	● For marinade, stir together salad dressing, soy sauce, wine, onion, lemon slices, dry mustard, and lemon-pepper seasoning. Pour marinade over meat in bag. Close bag. Marinate in the refrigerator for 6 to 24 hours, turning the bag several times.	
	● Drain steak, reserving the marinade. Grill flank steak on an uncovered grill directly over *medium* coals for 12 to 14 minutes or till medium-rare, turning once and brushing frequently with reserved marinade. To serve, diagonally slice meat across the grain into very thin slices. Makes 4 servings.	

Nutrition information per serving: 269 calories, 27 g protein, 1 g carbohydrate, 16 g fat, 73 mg cholesterol, 441 mg sodium, 452 mg potassium.

Spice-Rubbed Steak

1 teaspoon lemon-pepper seasoning ⅛ teaspoon salt ⅛ teaspoon ground nutmeg 2 beef rib eye steaks, cut 1 inch thick (about 1½ pounds total) 1 lime *or* lemon, cut into wedges	● Stir together lemon-pepper seasoning, salt, and nutmeg. Cut steaks into 4 equal portions. Rub lemon-pepper mixture on the steaks. Grill steaks on an uncovered grill directly over *medium-hot* coals to desired doneness, turning once. (Allow 8 to 12 minutes for rare, 12 to 15 minutes for medium, and 16 to 20 minutes for well-done.) Serve steak with lime or lemon wedges. Makes 4 servings.	**Have your dinner guests squeeze lime or lemon wedges over their steaks. The citrus juice accents the warm, piquant nutmeg.**

Nutrition information per serving: 231 calories, 24 g protein, 0 g carbohydrate, 14 g fat, 78 mg cholesterol, 287 mg sodium, 358 mg potassium.

Jalapeño and Apple Chops

1	10-ounce jar apple jelly
1	to 2 canned jalapeño chili peppers, chopped
¼	cup apple juice *or* orange juice
1	tablespoon cornstarch

● In a small saucepan combine jelly and jalapeño peppers. Cook and stir over low heat till jelly melts. Combine apple juice and cornstarch. Stir into jelly mixture. Cook and stir till thickened and bubbly. Cook and stir for 2 minutes more.

The sweetness of the apple jelly complements the hotness of the jalapeño peppers.

4	pork loin chops, cut 1¼ inches thick
2	apple slices, cut ½ inch thick, cored, and halved Parsley sprigs

● In a covered grill arrange preheated coals around drip pan. Test for *medium-slow* heat above pan. Place chops on rack over pan. Lower hood. Grill for 40 to 45 minutes or till well-done, turning once. Brush with jelly mixture during last 10 minutes of cooking.

   Meanwhile, wrap apple slices in foil. Place on side of grill during last 10 minutes of cooking. Serve atop chops. Spoon any remaining jelly mixture over all. Garnish with parsley. Serves 4.

Nutrition information per serving: 489 calories, 31 g protein, 56 g carbohydrate, 16 g fat, 102 mg cholesterol, 92 mg sodium, 522 mg potassium.

Mustard Pork Chops

½	teaspoon finely shredded orange peel
¼	cup orange juice
2	tablespoons cooking oil
2	tablespoons coarse-grain brown mustard
2	tablespoons Dijon-style mustard
1	tablespoon white wine vinegar *or* vinegar
½	teaspoon dry mustard
4	pork loin chops, cut 1¼ inches thick
2	tablespoons molasses

● For marinade, stir together orange peel, orange juice, cooking oil, brown mustard, Dijon-style mustard, vinegar, and dry mustard. Place chops in a plastic bag set into a shallow dish. Pour marinade over chops. Close bag. Marinate in the refrigerator for 6 to 24 hours, turning occasionally.

   Drain chops, reserving ⅓ *cup* of the marinade. Set aside. In a covered grill arrange preheated coals around drip pan. Test for *medium-slow* heat above pan. Place chops on rack over pan. Lower hood. Grill for 40 to 45 minutes or till well-done, turning once. Stir molasses into reserved marinade. Brush on chops often during last 10 minutes of cooking. Makes 4 servings.

Nutrition information per serving: 299 calories, 31 g protein, 2 g carbohydrate, 18 g fat, 102 mg cholesterol, 159 mg sodium, 456 mg potassium.

Serving Suggestion:
Zucchini and Carrots
   Tear off an 18x36-inch piece of heavy-duty foil. Fold in half to make a square. Fold up sides, using fist to make a pouch. In the pouch place 1 cup *zucchini* cut into ¼-inch-thick slices, 1 cup *carrots* cut into julienne strips, 1 tablespoon *margarine,* and ½ teaspoon finely shredded *orange peel.* Sprinkle with salt and pepper. Fold edges of foil to secure, leaving space for steam to build. Place on rack beside chops. Lower hood. Grill over coals for 20 minutes, turning occasionally.

Jalapeño and Apple Chops

Pineapple Lamb Chops

8 lamb rib chops, cut 1 inch thick (about 1½ pounds total)	● Trim excess fat from meat. Cut a pocket in each of the chops by cutting from fat side almost to the bone.
1 8¼-ounce can crushed pineapple ¾ cup cooked rice 1 tablespoon thinly sliced green onion ¼ teaspoon ground ginger ⅛ teaspoon salt	● For stuffing, drain pineapple, reserving syrup for the glaze. In a mixing bowl combine ⅓ cup of the drained pineapple (set aside remaining pineapple), cooked rice, green onion, ground ginger, and salt; toss lightly to mix. Spoon a generous 2 tablespoons stuffing into each pocket. Fasten pockets with wooden toothpicks, if necessary.
1 tablespoon honey 2 teaspoons soy sauce	● For glaze, combine ¼ cup of the reserved pineapple syrup, honey, and soy sauce. Brush some glaze over chops. Grill chops on an uncovered grill directly over medium coals for 7 minutes. Turn and grill to desired doneness, brushing once with the glaze. (Allow 7 to 9 minutes more for medium and 18 to 20 minutes more for well-done.)
1 teaspoon cornstarch	● In a small saucepan stir together remaining glaze, reserved crushed pineapple, and cornstarch. Cook and stir over medium heat till thickened and bubbly. Cook and stir 2 minutes more. If desired, stir in any remaining pineapple syrup to thin sauce. Serve over lamb chops. Makes 4 servings.

Nutrition information per serving: 292 calories, 25 g protein, 26 g carbohydrate, 9 g fat, 87 mg cholesterol, 297 mg sodium, 354 mg potassium.

Serving Suggestion:
Garlic Bread
Cut half of an 18-inch-long loaf of *French bread* into 1-inch slices, cutting to, but not through, the bottom crust. Reserve other half for another use. Stir together 2 tablespoons softened *margarine* or *butter* and ¼ teaspoon *garlic powder.* Thinly spread mixture between every other slice of bread. Wrap loosely in heavy-duty foil. Place on the grill rack beside the lamb chops. Grill over coals about 10 minutes or till heated through, turning frequently.

Orange-Chinese Chops

1 teaspoon finely shredded orange peel ½ cup orange juice 3 tablespoons Chinese rice wine *or* dry white wine 3 tablespoons soy sauce ½ teaspoon grated gingerroot ⅛ teaspoon ground red pepper	● For marinade, stir together orange peel, orange juice, Chinese rice wine or white wine, soy sauce, gingerroot, and ground red pepper.
2 pork loin chops, cut 1¼ inches thick	● Place chops in a plastic bag set into a shallow dish. Pour marinade over chops. Close bag. Marinate in the refrigerator for 6 to 24 hours, turning occasionally.
1 teaspoon cornstarch	● Drain pork chops, reserving marinade. Set aside ½ *cup* of the marinade for the sauce. In a covered grill arrange preheated coals around a drip pan. Test for *medium-slow* heat above the drip pan. Place chops on the grill rack over the drip pan but not over the coals. Lower grill hood. Grill for 40 to 45 minutes or till chops are well-done, brushing occasionally with remaining marinade. 　　Meanwhile, for sauce, stir together the ½ cup reserved marinade and cornstarch. Cook and stir till thickened and bubbly. Cook and stir for 2 minutes more. Serve atop chops. Serves 2.

Nutrition information per serving: 341 calories, 33 g protein, 11 g carbohydrate, 16 g fat, 102 mg cholesterol, 1,624 mg sodium, 657 mg potassium.

Get a double dose of a favorite Chinese flavor combination: orange and red pepper. Dose one comes when the meat marinates. Dose two comes when you use some of the marinade to make the sauce.

Pecan-Stuffed Pork Chops

4 pork loin rib chops, cut 1½ inches thick	● Cut a pocket in each chop by cutting from the fat side almost to the bone. Place chops in a plastic bag set into a shallow dish.
½ teaspoon finely shredded orange peel **½ cup orange juice** **¼ cup soy sauce**	● For marinade, combine orange peel, orange juice, and soy sauce. Pour over chops in bag. Close bag and marinate in the refrigerator for 6 to 24 hours, turning occasionally.
¼ cup finely chopped onion **¼ cup chopped celery** **1 tablespoon margarine *or* butter** **¼ cup orange juice** **¾ cup corn bread stuffing mix** **2 tablespoons chopped pecans**	● For stuffing, in a saucepan cook onion and celery in margarine or butter till tender. Stir in orange juice. Bring to boiling. Remove from heat. In a mixing bowl combine corn bread stuffing mix and pecans. Add the onion-orange-juice mixture, tossing lightly to mix.
	● Drain meat, reserving the marinade. Spoon stuffing into the pork chop pockets. Fasten pockets with wooden toothpicks.
	● In a covered grill arrange preheated coals around a drip pan. Test for *medium* heat above the pan. Place chops on the grill rack over the drip pan but not over the coals. Lower grill hood. Grill for 40 to 45 minutes or till well-done, turning once and brushing occasionally with reserved marinade. Serves 4.

Nutrition information per serving: 438 calories, 35 g protein, 24 g carbohydrate, 22 g fat, 103 mg cholesterol, 726 mg sodium, 576 mg potassium.

Garden-Stuffed Fish Steaks

1¼ to 1½ pounds fresh *or* frozen swordfish steaks, cut 1 inch thick

● Thaw fish, if frozen. Remove bones from steaks, if necessary. Cut steaks into 4 portions. Cut a pocket in each of the steak portions by cutting along one side almost through to the other side.

Fish steaks stuffed with garden vegetables are a perfect best-of-summer treat.

½ cup coarsely shredded carrot
¼ cup sliced green onion
1 clove garlic, minced
2 tablespoons margarine *or* butter
1 small tomato, seeded and chopped
2 tablespoons fine dry seasoned bread crumbs
2 tablespoons grated Parmesan cheese
¼ teaspoon dried marjoram, crushed

● For stuffing, in a small saucepan cook carrot, onion, and garlic in margarine or butter till tender. Remove from heat. Add tomato, bread crumbs, cheese, and marjoram. Toss lightly to mix. Spoon about ¼ *cup* stuffing into *each* pocket. Fasten pockets with wooden toothpicks.

Cooking oil
Lemon wedges (optional)

● Brush the grill rack or a wire grill basket with cooking oil. Grill steaks on an uncovered grill directly over *medium-hot* coals for 14 to 18 minutes or till fish flakes easily with a fork, turning once. Serve with lemon wedges, if desired. Makes 4 servings.

Nutrition information per serving: 253 calories, 28 g protein, 7 g carbohydrate, 12 g fat, 52 mg cholesterol, 279 mg sodium, 498 mg potassium.

Citrus Salmon Steaks

2 fresh *or* frozen salmon steaks, cut 1¼ inches thick
¼ cup dry white wine
2 teaspoons finely shredded lime *or* lemon peel
3 tablespoons lime *or* lemon juice
2 tablespoons cooking oil
2 cloves garlic, minced

● Thaw salmon, if frozen. Place in a shallow baking dish. For marinade, combine wine, lime or lemon peel, lime or lemon juice, cooking oil, garlic, and ¼ teaspoon *pepper*. Pour over salmon, turning salmon to coat with marinade. Cover dish. Marinate salmon in the refrigerator for 2 hours, turning once.

Trust your nose when you select fresh salmon. Avoid any fish with a strong or fishy odor. Also look for firm flesh with a moist, smooth surface.

Cooking oil
Lime *or* lemon wedges (optional)

● Drain salmon, reserving marinade. Brush grill rack or wire grill basket with cooking oil. Place salmon on rack or in basket. Brush with marinade. Grill on an uncovered grill directly over *medium-hot* coals for 12 to 16 minutes or till fish flakes easily, turning once and brushing with marinade. Serve with lime or lemon wedges. Makes 2 to 4 servings.

Nutrition information per serving: 371 calories, 35 g protein, 1 g carbohydrate, 24 g fat, 60 mg cholesterol, 114 mg sodium, 662 mg potassium.

Swordfish with Rosemary Butter

1¼ to 1½ pounds fresh *or* frozen swordfish steaks, cut 1 inch thick
¼ cup margarine *or* butter
2 teaspoons snipped fresh rosemary *or* ½ teaspoon dried rosemary, crushed
1 teaspoon lemon juice

● Thaw fish, if frozen. Meanwhile, in a small saucepan combine margarine or butter, fresh or dried rosemary, lemon juice, and ⅛ teaspoon *pepper*. Cook, stirring occasionally, till margarine or butter melts. Remove bones from steaks, if necessary.

Next time, try using fresh or dried dillweed in place of the rosemary.

Cooking oil

● Cut steaks into 4 portions. Brush grill rack or wire grill basket with oil. Place fish on rack or in basket. Grill on an uncovered grill directly over *medium-hot* coals for 12 to 16 minutes or till fish flakes easily, turning once and brushing with butter mixture. Pass remaining butter mixture. Serves 4.

Nutrition information per serving: 248 calories, 24 g protein, 0 g carbohydrate, 16 g fat, 47 mg cholesterol, 242 mg sodium, 354 mg potassium.

Basic Barbecue Sauce

1 cup catsup
½ cup water
¼ cup finely chopped onion
   or 1 tablespoon minced dried onion
¼ cup vinegar
1 to 2 tablespoons sugar *or* brown sugar
1 tablespoon Worcestershire sauce
¼ teaspoon salt
¼ teaspoon celery seed
2 to 3 dashes bottled hot pepper sauce

● In a saucepan combine catsup, water, onion, vinegar, sugar, Worcestershire sauce, salt, celery seed, and bottled hot pepper sauce. Bring to boiling. Reduce heat. Simmer, uncovered, for 10 to 15 minutes or to desired consistency. Makes about 1½ cups.

Nutrition information per tablespoon: 17 calories, 0 g protein, 4 g carbohydrate, 0 g fat, 0 mg cholesterol, 147 mg sodium, 45 mg potassium.

An all-purpose family-style barbecue sauce: not too hot, not too sweet, but just right.

Super-Fast Barbecue Sauce

¾ cup apricot preserves
½ cup bottled barbecue sauce
2 tablespoons soy sauce
1 tablespoon minced dried onion

● In a saucepan stir together preserves, barbecue sauce, soy sauce, and onion. Cook and stir over medium heat till heated through. Makes 1¼ cups.

Nutrition information per tablespoon: 39 calories, 0 g protein, 10 g carbohydrate, 0 g fat, 0 mg cholesterol, 155 mg sodium, 31 mg potassium.

Just stir together four ingredients and heat them through. You'll get great flavor without a long simmering time.

Honey-Beer Barbecue Sauce

1	small onion, chopped
1	clove garlic, minced
1	tablespoon cooking oil

● In a saucepan cook the chopped onion and minced garlic in cooking oil till the onion is tender.

You'll find just a touch of sweetness in this finger-lickin' sauce.

¾	cup chili sauce
½	cup beer
¼	cup honey
2	tablespoons Worcestershire sauce
1	tablespoon prepared mustard

● Stir in the chili sauce, beer, honey, Worcestershire sauce, and mustard. Bring mixture to boiling. Reduce heat. Simmer, uncovered, for 20 to 25 minutes or to desired consistency, stirring occasionally. Makes about 1½ cups.

Nutrition information per tablespoon: 28 calories, 0 g protein, 5 g carbohydrate, 1 g fat, 0 mg cholesterol, 124 mg sodium, 35 mg potassium.

Fiery-Hot Barbecue Sauce

1 small onion, chopped
1 clove garlic, minced
1 tablespoon cooking oil

● In a saucepan cook chopped onion and minced garlic in cooking oil till onion is tender.

1½ cups catsup
⅓ cup vinegar
¼ cup molasses
1 tablespoon bottled hot
  pepper sauce
2 teaspoons ground red
  pepper
1 teaspoon chili powder
½ teaspoon salt
½ teaspoon dry mustard

● Stir in catsup, vinegar, molasses, hot pepper sauce, red pepper, chili powder, salt, and mustard. Bring mixture to boiling. Reduce heat. Simmer, uncovered, about 15 minutes or to desired consistency, stirring occasionally. Makes about 2 cups.

Nutrition information per tablespoon: 25 calories, 0 g protein, 5 g carbohydrate, 1 g fat, 0 mg cholesterol, 171 mg sodium, 81 mg potassium.

Keep a jar of this special sauce on hand in the refrigerator. Your hot-food-loving friends will think it's the best.

Spicy Barbecue Sauce

1 cup catsup
½ cup water
¼ cup finely chopped onion
  or 1 tablespoon dried minced onion
¼ cup vinegar
1 clove garlic, minced
1 teaspoon sugar
½ teaspoon ground coriander
¼ teaspoon salt
¼ teaspoon ground cumin
⅛ teaspoon ground ginger
⅛ teaspoon pepper

● In a saucepan combine catsup, water, onion, vinegar, garlic, sugar, coriander, salt, cumin, ground ginger, and pepper. Bring to boiling. Reduce heat. Simmer, uncovered, for 10 to 12 minutes or to desired consistency. Makes about 1⅓ cups.

Nutrition information per tablespoon: 16 calories, 0 g protein, 4 g carbohydrate, 0 g fat, 0 mg cholesterol, 161 mg sodium, 53 mg potassium.

Coriander, cumin, ginger, and pepper combine to create a perfectly seasoned barbecue sauce.

Tangy Barbecue Sauce

1 cup catsup
⅓ cup vinegar
⅓ cup corn syrup
¼ cup finely chopped onion
  or 1 tablespoon dried minced onion
1 tablespoon lemon juice
¼ teaspoon salt
  Several dashes bottled hot pepper sauce

● In a saucepan combine catsup, vinegar, corn syrup, chopped onion, lemon juice, salt, and bottled hot pepper sauce. Bring to boiling. Reduce heat. Simmer mixture, uncovered, for 10 to 15 minutes or to desired consistency. Makes about 1 cup.

Nutrition information per tablespoon: 40 calories, 0 g protein, 10 g carbohydrate, 0 g fat, 0 mg cholesterol, 215 mg sodium, 68 mg potassium.

Tangy versus sweet is often the issue in barbecue-sauce debates. This sauce, with its combination of vinegar and lemon juice, is designed to satisfy the tangy advocates.

Barbecue-Sauce Burgers

2 tablespoons homemade barbecue sauce (see recipes, pages 20–23) *or* bottled barbecue sauce
2 tablespoons fine dry bread crumbs
1 pound lean ground beef

● In a mixing bowl combine barbecue sauce, bread crumbs, and dash *pepper*. Add ground beef; mix well. Shape into four ¾-inch-thick patties.

Homemade barbecue sauce (see recipes, pages 20–23) *or* bottled barbecue sauce

● Grill patties on an uncovered grill directly over *medium-hot* coals for 15 to 18 minutes or till well-done, turning patties once and brushing frequently with barbecue sauce.

4 hamburger buns, split and toasted
4 lettuce leaves
Homemade barbecue sauce (see recipes, pages 20–23) *or* bottled barbecue sauce (optional)

● Serve patties on hamburger buns with lettuce leaves. Pass additional barbecue sauce, if desired. Makes 4 servings.

Nutrition information per serving: 374 calories, 24 g protein, 25 g carbohydrate, 19 g fat, 79 mg cholesterol, 370 mg sodium, 296 mg potassium.

Serving Suggestion:
Cheesy Corn
   Tear off an 18x36-inch piece of heavy-duty foil. Fold in half to make a square. Fold up sides to form a pouch. Combine one 17-ounce can *cream-style corn*, ½ cup shredded *American cheese*, ¼ cup crushed *rich round crackers*, 1 tablespoon *chopped pimiento*, and 1 teaspoon *minced dried onion*. Spoon into pouch. Fold edges to seal, leaving space for steam to build. Place on grill rack beside burgers. Grill over coals for **12 to 15 minutes** or till heated through, turning once.

Lamb Burgers

Pictured on page 27.

1	beaten egg
¼	cup fine dry bread crumbs
¼	cup finely chopped, seeded cucumber
2	tablespoons plain yogurt
1	clove garlic, minced
¼	teaspoon ground cumin
1	pound lean ground lamb

● In a bowl combine egg, bread crumbs, cucumber, yogurt, garlic, and cumin. Add lamb; mix well. Shape mixture into four ½-inch-thick oval patties (about 5 inches long). Grill on an uncovered grill directly over *medium-hot* coals for 13 to 16 minutes or till well-done, turning once.

2	large pita bread rounds, halved
8	thin cucumber slices
¼	cup shredded carrot
¼	cup plain yogurt

● Serve meat patties in pita halves with cucumber slices, shredded carrot, and yogurt. Makes 4 servings.

Nutrition information per serving: 304 calories, 27 g protein, 30 g carbohydrate, 8 g fat, 136 mg cholesterol, 129 mg sodium, 348 mg potassium.

You can't fit a square peg into a round hole. And you can't fit a round burger into an oval-shaped pita bread half. To make the burger and bread work together, shape the meat mixture into oval patties.

Cheese-Sauced Burgers

Pictured on page 27.

1	beaten egg
⅓	cup quick-cooking rolled oats
¼	cup catsup
½	teaspoon onion salt
	Dash pepper
1½	pounds lean ground beef

● In a bowl stir together egg, rolled oats, catsup, onion salt, and pepper. Add ground beef; mix well. Shape into six ¾-inch-thick patties. Grill on an uncovered grill directly over *medium-hot* coals for 15 to 18 minutes or till well-done, turning once.

1	8-ounce jar cheese spread with jalapeño peppers
2	tablespoons milk
3	English muffins, split and toasted
	Sliced green onion

● In a small saucepan combine cheese spread and milk. Cook over low heat, stirring frequently, till cheese melts. Serve patties on muffin halves. Pour cheese sauce atop. Sprinkle with green onion. Makes 6 servings.

Nutrition information per serving: 461 calories, 31 g protein, 25 g carbohydrate, 26 g fat, 143 mg cholesterol, 869 mg sodium, 390 mg potassium.

Some restaurants call them rarebit burgers; we call them Cheese-Sauced Burgers. By either name, these moist burgers, with their gobs of savory sauce, are sure to delight cheese lovers.

Aloha Turkey Burgers

1	8¼-ounce can pineapple slices
1	tablespoon prepared mustard
2	teaspoons sugar
1	teaspoon cornstarch
1	tablespoon margarine *or* butter

● Drain pineapple, reserving syrup. Wrap pineapple in heavy-duty foil; set aside. For sauce, in a saucepan combine prepared mustard, sugar, and cornstarch. Stir in reserved pineapple syrup. Cook and stir till thickened and bubbly. Cook and stir for 2 minutes more. Stir in margarine or butter. Keep warm.

Say "aloha" to these positively tropical, pineapple-topped burgers.

1	beaten egg
½	cup soft bread crumbs
¼	cup finely chopped celery
¼	teaspoon salt
¼	teaspoon ground ginger
⅛	teaspoon pepper
1	pound ground raw turkey
	Cooking oil

● Combine egg, crumbs, celery, salt, ginger, and pepper. Add turkey; mix well. Shape into four ¾-inch-thick patties. Brush cooking oil on grill basket. Place patties in basket. Grill on an uncovered grill directly over *medium-hot* coals for 15 to 18 minutes or till well-done, turning once and brushing often with sauce. Place pineapple on grill rack during last 5 minutes of cooking.

| 4 | slices French bread, toasted |
| | Parsley sprigs (optional) |

● Top each slice of French bread with a patty and a pineapple slice. Spoon any remaining sauce over all. Garnish with parsley sprigs, if desired. Makes 4 servings.

Nutrition information per serving: 367 calories, 31 g protein, 38 g carbohydrate, 10 g fat, 135 mg cholesterol, 522 mg sodium, 403 mg potassium.

Sour Cream Burgers
(see recipe, page 29)

Salmon Sandwiches
(see recipe, page 29)

Aloha Turkey Burgers

Pizza-Style Burgers

Pizza-Style Burgers

½ cup soft bread crumbs
1 8-ounce can pizza sauce
2 tablespoons grated Parmesan cheese
¼ teaspoon pepper
1 pound lean ground beef
2 ounces pepperoni, finely chopped

● Combine bread crumbs, *2 tablespoons* of the pizza sauce, Parmesan cheese, and pepper. Add beef and pepperoni; mix well. Shape into four ¾-inch-thick patties. Grill on an uncovered grill directly over *medium-hot* coals for 15 to 18 minutes or till well-done, turning once.

If you love pizza, you'll love these burgers. All of your favorite pizza flavors are mixed right into the meat.

2 slices mozzarella cheese
4 hamburger buns, split and toasted

● Meanwhile, heat remaining pizza sauce. Cut cheese slices into 8 triangles. Serve patties on buns with cheese. Pass remaining pizza sauce. Makes 4 servings.

Nutrition information per serving: 526 calories, 32 g protein, 31 g carbohydrate, 29 g fat, 100 mg cholesterol, 1,019 mg sodium, 543 mg potassium.

Cheese-Sauced Burgers
(see recipe, page 25)

Lamb Burgers
(see recipe, page 25)

Sausage-Pepper Burgers

½ pound lean ground pork
½ pound bulk pork sausage
1 4-ounce can diced green chili peppers, drained

● In a mixing bowl combine ground pork, sausage, and chili peppers; mix well. Shape into four ¾-inch-thick patties. Grill on an uncovered grill directly over *medium-hot* coals for 15 to 18 minutes or till patties are well-done, turning once.

4 hamburger buns, split and toasted
4 lettuce leaves
Taco sauce (optional)

● Serve patties on hamburger buns with lettuce leaves and, if desired, taco sauce. Makes 4 servings.

Nutrition information per serving: 298 calories, 22 g protein, 23 g carbohydrate, 13 g fat, 66 mg cholesterol, 831 mg sodium, 427 mg potassium.

These patties also are great for brunch. Just shape and grill the meat mixture, leaving off the buns, lettuce, and taco sauce.

Currant-Glazed Pork Burgers

¼ cup currant jelly
3 tablespoons catsup
1 tablespoon vinegar
⅛ teaspoon ground cinnamon
Dash ground cloves

● For sauce, in a small saucepan combine jelly, catsup, vinegar, cinnamon, and cloves. Cook and stir just till boiling. Keep warm.

1 beaten egg
3 tablespoons fine dry bread crumbs
2 tablespoons milk
2 tablespoons chopped onion
¼ teaspoon dried thyme, crushed
1 pound lean ground pork

● In a mixing bowl combine egg, fine dry bread crumbs, milk, chopped onion, thyme, ¼ teaspoon *salt*, and ⅛ teaspoon *pepper*. Add ground pork; mix well. Shape the meat mixture into four ¾-inch-thick patties.

4 English muffins, split and toasted
4 lettuce leaves

● Grill patties on an uncovered grill directly over *medium-hot* coals for 15 to 18 minutes or till well-done, turning once. Serve on toasted English muffins with lettuce leaves. Spoon sauce over the patties. Makes 4 servings.

Nutrition information per serving: 409 calories, 36 g protein, 52 g carbohydrate, 6 g fat, 153 mg cholesterol, 386 mg sodium, 599 mg potassium.

Serving Suggestion:
Molasses Beans
    Tear off an 18x36-inch piece of heavy-duty foil. Fold in half to form a square. Fold up sides, using your fist to form a pouch. Stir together one 16-ounce can *pork and beans in tomato sauce,* 2 tablespoons *molasses,* 2 tablespoons *cooked bacon pieces,* and 1 teaspoon *minced dried onion.* Spoon into pouch. Fold edges of foil to secure, leaving space for steam to build. Place on the grill rack beside the burgers. Grill over coals about 14 minutes or till heated through.

Sour Cream Burgers

Pictured on page 26.

1 beaten egg ¼ cup fine dry bread crumbs ¼ cup sour cream dip with French onion 1 pound lean ground beef	● In a mixing bowl combine egg, bread crumbs, sour cream dip, ¼ teaspoon *salt*, and dash *pepper*. Add ground beef; mix well. Shape into four ¾-inch-thick patties.
	● Grill patties on an uncovered grill directly over *medium-hot* coals for 15 to 18 minutes or till patties are well-done, turning once.
½ cup sour cream dip with French onion 1 small tomato, seeded and chopped 2 hamburger buns, split and toasted 4 lettuce leaves 1 small avocado, peeled, seeded, and sliced (optional)	● Stir together the sour cream dip and tomato. Serve patties on bun halves with lettuce leaves. Dollop with sour cream dip mixture. Garnish each patty with avocado slices, if desired. Serves 4. Nutrition information per serving: 403 calories, 29 g protein, 20 g carbohydrate, 22 g fat, 170 mg cholesterol, 716 mg sodium, 454 mg potassium.

Not just for potato chips, sour cream dip also is good mixed in and on top of burgers.

Salmon Sandwiches

Pictured on page 26.

1 beaten egg 1 tablespoon milk 1 tablespoon Dijon-style mustard ½ teaspoon dried dillweed ½ cup finely crushed rich round crackers 1 15½-ounce can salmon, drained, flaked, and skin and bones removed	● In a mixing bowl combine egg, milk, Dijon-style mustard, and dried dillweed. Stir in crushed crackers. Add salmon; mix well. Shape mixture into four ½-inch-thick patties.
Cooking oil	● Brush the grill rack with cooking oil. Grill patties on an uncovered grill directly over *medium-hot* coals for 12 to 14 minutes or till brown, turning once.
¼ cup dairy sour cream 1 tablespoon Dijon-style mustard 4 hamburger buns, split and toasted 4 lettuce leaves 4 tomato slices	● Stir together sour cream and Dijon-style mustard. Serve salmon patties on buns with lettuce and tomato. Dollop with sour cream mixture. Serves 4. Nutrition information per serving: 399 calories, 24 g protein, 30 g carbohydrate, 19 g fat, 109 mg cholesterol, 612 mg sodium, 485 mg potassium.

For these easy burgers, choose the least expensive salmon varieties available (chum or pink). They'll give you all the flavor and color you need without the extra expense.

Bacon-Beef Burger Dogs

1 beaten egg ¼ cup fine dry bread crumbs 3 tablespoons sweet pickle relish 2 tablespoons catsup 1 pound lean ground beef	● In a mixing bowl combine egg, fine dry bread crumbs, relish, catsup, and dash *pepper*. Add ground beef; mix well.
6 slices bacon 3 frankfurters, halved lengthwise	● In a skillet cook bacon till nearly done but not crisp. Shape *one-sixth* of the meat mixture around *each* frankfurter half. Wrap *one* slice of bacon around *each;* secure with wooden toothpicks. Grill on an uncovered grill directly over *medium-hot* coals for 14 to 16 minutes or till well-done, turning often.
6 frankfurter buns, split and toasted Sweet pickle relish Catsup Mustard	● Serve on frankfurter buns with relish, catsup, and mustard. Makes 6 servings. Nutrition information per serving: 449 calories, 27 g protein, 34 g carbohydrate, 22 g fat, 122 mg cholesterol, 1,073 mg sodium, 405 mg potassium.

Can't decide between a hamburger and a hot dog? Your problem is solved. We rolled them both into one fantastic sandwich.

'Ham' Burgers

1 tablespoon brown sugar 2 teaspoons cornstarch 1 6-ounce can (¾ cup) apricot nectar 1 tablespoon vinegar	● For sauce, combine sugar and cornstarch. Stir in ½ *cup* of the apricot nectar and vinegar. Cook and stir till thickened and bubbly. Cook and stir 2 minutes more. Keep warm.
1 beaten egg ½ cup corn bread stuffing mix ¼ cup sliced green onion 1 pound ground fully cooked ham 1 pound ground pork	● In a mixing bowl combine egg, stuffing mix, onion, remaining nectar, and dash *pepper*. Add ground ham and pork; mix well. Shape the meat mixture into eight ¾-inch-thick patties.
	● Grill patties on an uncovered grill directly over *medium-hot* coals for 15 to 18 minutes or till well-done, turning the patties once.
8 hamburger buns, split and toasted 8 lettuce leaves	● Serve patties on hamburger buns with lettuce leaves. Spoon sauce atop patties. Makes 8 servings. Nutrition information per serving: 342 calories, 30 g protein, 35 g carbohydrate, 9 g fat, 109 mg cholesterol, 1,042 mg sodium, 514 mg potassium.

Serving Suggestion:
Roasted Corn on the Cob Stir together ½ cup softened *margarine* or *butter*, 1 teaspoon *chili powder*, and ½ teaspoon *salt*. Turn back husks of 8 ears of *corn;* remove silks with a stiff brush. Place each ear on a piece of heavy-duty foil. Spread corn with the margarine mixture. Replace husks. Wrap foil around corn. Place foil packets on the grill rack beside the burgers. Grill over coals for 15 to 18 minutes or till tender, turning occasionally.

Stuffed American Burgers

Pictured on page 35.

2 tablespoons catsup 1 tablespoon prepared 　　mustard 1 pound lean ground beef	● In a bowl combine catsup, mustard, ¼ teaspoon *salt,* and ⅛ teaspoon *pepper.* Add beef; mix well. Shape into eight ¼-inch-thick patties.
12 slices dill pickle 4 slices American cheese	● Top *four* of the patties with pickle slices. Top with remaining beef patties. Seal edges. Grill on an uncovered grill directly over *medium-hot* coals for 15 to 18 minutes or till well-done, turning once. Top each patty with a cheese slice for the last 2 minutes of grilling.
4 hamburger buns, split and 　　toasted 4 lettuce leaves 4 tomato slices	● Serve the patties on toasted hamburger buns with lettuce and tomato. Pass additional catsup and mustard, if desired. Makes 4 servings.

Nutrition information per serving: 428 calories, 33 g protein, 25 g carbohydrate, 21 g fat, 109 mg cholesterol, 1,149 mg sodium, 450 mg potassium.

These all-American burgers combine favorite American condiments. Catsup and mustard are mixed with the meat, dill pickle hides inside the burgers, and cheese tops them all.

Bratwursts in Beer

6 fresh bratwursts (about 1¼ 　　pounds total) 3 12-ounce cans (4½ cups) 　　beer	● Prick several holes in the skin of each bratwurst (see photo, right). In a Dutch oven combine bratwursts and beer. Bring to boiling. Reduce heat. Simmer, covered, about 20 minutes or till bratwursts are no longer pink. Drain.
	● Grill bratwursts on an uncovered grill directly over *medium-hot* coals for 7 to 8 minutes or till the bratwurst skins are golden, turning frequently.
6 frankfurter buns, split and 　　toasted 　　Various mustards 　　Catsup 1 8-ounce can sauerkraut, 　　drained (optional)	● Serve bratwursts on buns with mustards, catsup, and, if desired, sauerkraut. Makes 6 servings.

Nutrition information per serving: 494 calories, 15 g protein, 25 g carbohydrate, 24 g fat, 53 mg cholesterol, 679 mg sodium, 229 mg potassium.

Use the tines of a fork to prick the bratwursts before boiling them. This allows the fat to cook out.

Mexican-Style Burgers

Pictured on page 35.

1 beaten egg
1 4-ounce can diced green
  chili peppers, drained
⅓ cup finely crushed tortilla
  chips
2 tablespoons chopped
  onion
2 tablespoons taco sauce
1 clove garlic, minced
¼ teaspoon salt
1½ pounds lean ground beef

● In a mixing bowl combine egg, chili peppers, tortilla chips, onion, taco sauce, garlic, and salt. Add beef; mix well. Shape the meat mixture into six ¾-inch-thick patties.

Get out the sombreros and maracas! The flavor of these burgers will remind dinner guests of a trip south of the border (or, at least, to the corner Mexican restaurant).

● Grill patties on an uncovered grill directly over *medium-hot* coals for 15 to 18 minutes or till well-done, turning the patties once.

6 10-inch flour tortillas

● Meanwhile, wrap tortillas in foil. Heat in a 400° oven about 10 minutes or till warm, turning once. (Or, heat wrapped tortillas on the edge of the grill, but not over the coals, for 5 to 7 minutes or till warm, turning once.)

1 medium tomato, chopped
1 cup shredded Monterey
  Jack cheese, Monterey
  Jack cheese with
  jalapeño peppers, *or*
  cheddar cheese
¾ cup shredded lettuce
  Taco sauce

● Place meat patties on warmed tortillas. Top with chopped tomato, shredded cheese, and shredded lettuce. Wrap tortillas around patties. Pass taco sauce. Makes 6 servings.

Nutrition information per serving: 428 calories, 33 g protein, 33 g carbohydrate, 18 g fat, 142 mg cholesterol, 603 mg sodium, 417 mg potassium.

Oriental Beef Burgers

½ cup cooked rice
¼ cup chopped water
    chestnuts
2 tablespoons sliced green
    onion
2 tablespoons soy sauce
1 clove garlic, minced
¼ teaspoon five-spice
    powder
1 pound lean ground beef

● In a mixing bowl combine rice, water chestnuts, onion, soy sauce, garlic, five-spice powder, and ¼ teaspoon *pepper*. Add ground beef; mix well. Shape into four ¾-inch-thick patties. Grill on an uncovered grill directly over *medium-hot* coals for 15 to 18 minutes or till well-done, turning once.

Get the best of both worlds. The burger is American, but the flavor is purely Oriental.

4 hamburger buns, split and
    toasted
4 fresh spinach *or* Chinese
    cabbage leaves

● Serve patties on hamburger buns with fresh spinach or Chinese cabbage leaves. Makes 4 servings.

Nutrition information per serving: 405 calories, 25 g protein, 32 g carbohydrate, 19 g fat, 79 mg cholesterol, 773 mg sodium, 410 mg potassium.

Stuffed American Burgers
(see recipe, page 32)

Mexican-Style Burgers
(see recipe, page 33)

Oriental Beef Burgers

Hot Pear Relish

Sauerkraut Relish

Hot Pear Relish

4 medium pears, peeled and finely chopped (4 cups)
4 cups cider vinegar
4 large green peppers, finely chopped (3 cups)
3 large onions, finely chopped (3 cups)
2 cups sugar
3 jalapeño peppers, seeded and finely chopped
2 tablespoons prepared mustard
1½ teaspoons ground turmeric

● In a 5-quart kettle or Dutch oven combine pears, vinegar, green peppers, onions, sugar, jalapeño peppers, mustard, and turmeric. Bring to boiling; reduce heat. Simmer, uncovered, about 1 hour or till thick, stirring occasionally.

Pack hot pear mixture into hot, clean ½-pint canning jars, leaving a ½-inch headspace. Wipe jar rims; adjust lids. Process in a boiling-water bath for 10 minutes (start timing when water boils). Serve on burgers or sausages. Makes 6 half-pints.

Nutrition information per tablespoon: 25 calories, 0 g protein, 6 g carbohydrate, 0 g fat, 0 mg cholesterol, 4 mg sodium, 42 mg potassium.

Protect yourself when handling jalapeño peppers. Wear gloves and avoid touching your eyes and skin.

Sauerkraut Relish

3 tablespoons vinegar
1 tablespoon sugar
1 teaspoon pickling spice
1 teaspoon caraway seed
1 8-ounce can sauerkraut, rinsed and drained
¼ cup finely chopped sweet red *or* green pepper

● Combine vinegar and sugar. Cook and stir till sugar is dissolved. Stir in pickling spice and caraway. Stir in sauerkraut and pepper. Cover and chill till serving time. Serve on burgers or sausages. Makes about 1 cup.

Nutrition information per tablespoon: 6 calories, 0 g protein, 2 g carbohydrate, 0 g fat, 0 mg cholesterol, 68 mg sodium, 21 mg potassium.

Use this relish to add a little German flavor to your bratwursts, burgers, or other sandwiches.

**Sambal
Condiment**

Quick Corn
Relish

Sambal Condiment

2 fresh hot red peppers
2 fresh hot green peppers
2 medium tomatoes, peeled, seeded, and finely chopped
¼ cup finely chopped shallot *or* green onion
1 teaspoon finely shredded lime peel
¼ cup lime juice

● Cut peppers open. Discard stems and seeds. Finely chop peppers. In a small bowl combine the peppers, tomatoes, shallot or green onion, lime peel, and juice. Cover and chill till serving time. Serve on burgers or sausages. Makes about 1¼ cups.

Nutrition information per tablespoon: 7 calories, 0 g protein, 2 g carbohydrate, 0 g fat, 0 mg cholesterol, 1 mg sodium, 55 mg potassium.

Patterned after an Indonesian favorite, this relish adds a tangy hotness to sandwiches.

Quick Corn Relish

2 tablespoons sugar
1 teaspoon cornstarch
3 tablespoons vinegar
2 tablespoons water
1 tablespoon dried minced onion
1 12-ounce can whole kernel corn with sweet peppers, drained
¼ cup mustard-style hot dog relish

● In a saucepan combine sugar and cornstarch. Stir in vinegar, water, and onion. Cook and stir till thickened and bubbly. Cook and stir 2 minutes more. Stir in the drained corn and relish. Transfer to a bowl. Cover and chill till serving time. Serve on burgers or sausages. Makes about 1⅔ cups.

Nutrition information per tablespoon: 14 calories, 0 g protein, 4 g carbohydrate, 0 g fat, 0 mg cholesterol, 42 mg sodium, 23 mg potassium.

Relish how easy it is to make this relish!

Chinese Smoked Ribs

4 cups hickory chips
4 pounds pork loin back ribs
   or spareribs
2 tablespoons sugar
½ teaspoon salt
½ teaspoon paprika
½ teaspoon ground turmeric
¼ teaspoon celery seed
⅛ teaspoon dry mustard

● At least 1 hour before cooking, soak wood chips in enough water to cover. Drain. Meanwhile, cut ribs into serving-size pieces. Place in a Dutch oven. Add enough water to cover. Bring to boiling. Reduce heat. Simmer, covered, for 30 minutes. Drain.

Stir together sugar, salt, paprika, turmeric, celery seed, and mustard. Thoroughly rub ribs with spice mixture.

½ cup packed brown sugar
½ cup catsup
3 tablespoons soy sauce
1 tablespoon grated
   gingerroot *or* 2
   teaspoons ground
   ginger
1 clove garlic, minced

● For sauce, combine brown sugar, catsup, soy sauce, gingerroot or ginger, and garlic. Cook and stir over low heat till sugar is dissolved.

In a covered grill arrange preheated coals around a drip pan. Test for *slow* heat above the pan. Pour 1 inch of water into the drip pan. Place drained wood chips on top of coals. Place ribs on grill rack over the drip pan but not over the coals. Lower grill hood. Grill about 45 minutes or till ribs are tender, brushing with sauce occasionally. Heat any remaining sauce and serve with ribs. Makes 4 servings.

Nutrition information per serving: 879 calories, 53 g protein, 43 g carbohydrate, 54 g fat, 214 mg cholesterol, 1,568 mg sodium, 857 mg potassium.

For an appetizer, cut the ribs into single-rib portions and cook as directed. You can plan on having 16 to 20 mini-portions.

Ribs in Beer Sauce

4 pounds beef short ribs	● Place ribs in a Dutch oven. Add enough water to cover. Bring to boiling. Reduce heat. Simmer, covered, for 1½ hours. Drain ribs.	**Add a touch of hotness to the sauce with a few dashes of bottled hot pepper sauce.**
½ cup bottled chili sauce **⅓ cup beer** **1 tablespoon prepared mustard** **¼ teaspoon pepper**	● Meanwhile, for sauce, stir together chili sauce, beer, mustard, and pepper. In a covered grill arrange preheated coals around a drip pan. Test for *slow* heat above the pan. Pour 1 inch of water into the drip pan. Place ribs on the grill rack over the drip pan but not over the coals. Lower grill hood. Grill for 20 to 30 minutes or till the ribs are tender, turning and brushing with sauce occasionally. Heat and pass any remaining sauce. Serves 4. Nutrition information per serving: 404 calories, 49 g protein, 10 g carbohydrate, 17 g fat, 147 mg cholesterol, 589 mg sodium, 520 mg potassium.	

Honey-Ginger-Glazed Ribs

4 pounds pork loin back ribs *or* pork country-style ribs	● Cut ribs into serving-size pieces. Place in a Dutch oven. Add enough water to cover. Bring to boiling. Reduce heat. Simmer, covered, for 30 minutes. Drain.	**Don't have white wine on hand? Use 1 tablespoon vinegar and 3 tablespoons water instead.**
½ cup honey **¼ cup dry white wine** **2 tablespoons Dijon-style mustard** **1 tablespoon cornstarch** **¼ teaspoon ground ginger** **⅛ teaspoon ground allspice**	● For sauce, stir together honey, wine, mustard, cornstarch, ginger, and allspice. Cook and stir till sauce is thickened and bubbly. Cook and stir for 2 minutes more. In a covered grill arrange preheated coals around a drip pan. Test for *slow* heat above pan. Pour 1 inch of water into pan. Place ribs on rack over pan but not over coals. Lower hood. Grill about 45 minutes or till tender, brushing with sauce often. Makes 4 servings. Nutrition information per serving: 860 calories, 52 g protein, 37 g carbohydrate, 54 g fat, 214 mg cholesterol, 388 mg sodium, 611 mg potassium.	

Barbecued Ribs with Fig Sauce

3 pounds meaty pork spareribs *or* pork loin back ribs	● If desired, cut the ribs into serving-size pieces. Place in a Dutch oven. Add enough water to cover the ribs. Bring to boiling. Reduce heat. Simmer, covered, for 30 minutes. Drain. Sprinkle with salt and pepper.
1 17-ounce can figs 3 tablespoons soy sauce 3 tablespoons vinegar ¾ teaspoon dry mustard ½ teaspoon ground ginger *or* 1 teaspoon grated gingerroot ¼ cup sliced green onion	● Meanwhile, for sauce, drain figs, reserving *½ cup* of the syrup. In a blender container or food processor bowl combine reserved fig syrup, figs, soy sauce, vinegar, dry mustard, and ginger or gingerroot. Cover and blend or process till mixture is smooth. Pour fig mixture into a saucepan. Stir in green onion. Bring to boiling. Reduce heat. Simmer, covered, for 5 to 10 minutes or to desired consistency.
	● Place ribs in a rib rack, if desired. In a covered grill arrange preheated coals around a drip pan. Test for *slow* heat above the pan. Pour 1 inch of water into the pan. Place ribs on the grill rack over the drip pan but not over the coals. Brush ribs with sauce. Lower hood. Grill about 45 minutes or till tender, brushing with sauce occasionally. Heat and pass any remaining sauce. Makes 3 servings.

Nutrition information per serving: 863 calories, 54 g protein, 40 g carbohydrate, 54 g fat, 214 mg cholesterol, 1,196 mg sodium, 811 mg potassium.

Garnish the platter of ribs with orange slices or kumquat flowers.

A rib rack isn't necessary to grill ribs, but it's a nice convenience. Just place whole or halved slabs of ribs in the rib rack, then place the rack on the grill rack above the drip pan. Grill as directed in the recipe.

Spiced Molasses Ribs

4 pounds pork loin back ribs *or* **meaty pork spareribs**	● Cut ribs into serving-size pieces. Place in a Dutch oven. Add enough water to cover ribs. Bring to boiling. Reduce heat. Simmer, covered, for 30 minutes. Drain ribs. Sprinkle with salt and pepper.	**Keep your kitchen cool by using your microwave to start the ribs.**
¼ cup prepared mustard **¼ cup molasses** **⅓ cup pineapple preserves** **3 tablespoons vinegar** **1 teaspoon five-spice powder**	● Meanwhile, for sauce, in a saucepan stir together prepared mustard and molasses. Stir in pineapple preserves, vinegar, and five-spice powder. Cook and stir till the pineapple preserves melt. Keep warm.	
	● In a covered grill arrange preheated coals around a drip pan. Test for *slow* heat above pan. Pour 1 inch of water into pan. Place ribs on rack over the drip pan but not over the coals. Lower grill hood. Grill about 45 minutes or till tender, brushing with the sauce occasionally. Heat and pass any remaining sauce. Makes 4 servings.	

● **Microwave directions:** Omit simmering ribs in water. Arrange *half* of the ribs in a 12x7½x2-inch microwave-safe baking dish, overlapping as necessary. Cover with vented microwave-safe plastic wrap. Micro-cook ribs on 100% power (high) for 10 minutes. Drain off fat. Rearrange and turn ribs over, exposing the less-cooked pieces and overlapping the more-cooked portions. Cook, covered, on high for 5 to 10 minutes more or till no pink remains. Drain ribs; sprinkle with salt and pepper. Set aside. Repeat with remaining half of ribs. Prepare sauce and grill ribs as above.

Nutrition information per serving: 837 calories, 52 g protein, 33 g carbohydrate, 54 g fat, 214 mg cholesterol, 363 mg sodium, 837 mg potassium.

Sonoma Beef Ribs

2½ pounds beef short ribs
1 teaspoon dried rosemary, crushed
1 bay leaf

● Place ribs in a Dutch oven. Add enough water to cover. Sprinkle with rosemary and add bay leaf. Bring to boiling. Reduce heat. Simmer, covered, for 1½ hours. Drain.

1 medium onion, chopped
1 small green pepper, chopped
1 tablespoon cooking oil
½ cup tomato sauce
½ cup plum or grape jelly
2 tablespoons vinegar
1 tablespoon chili powder
1 teaspoon Worcestershire sauce

● Meanwhile, for sauce, in a saucepan, cook onion and green pepper in cooking oil till tender. Stir in tomato sauce, jelly, vinegar, chili powder, and Worcestershire sauce. Bring to boiling. Reduce heat; simmer, covered, for 20 minutes.

● In a covered grill arrange preheated coals around drip pan. Test for *slow* heat above pan. Pour 1 inch of water into pan. Brush ribs with sauce. Place ribs on rack over pan. Lower hood. Grill for 20 to 30 minutes or till tender, turning and brushing with sauce often. Pass any remaining sauce. Makes 4 servings.

Nutrition information per serving: 424 calories, 36 g protein, 34 g carbohydrate, 16 g fat, 106 mg cholesterol, 281 mg sodium, 548 mg potassium.

Serving Suggestion:
Sherried Dessert Peaches
Stir together ⅓ cup *cream sherry* or *port,* 3 tablespoons *sugar,* 2 tablespoons *apricot preserves* or *peach preserves,* 1 tablespoon *lemon juice,* and ⅛ teaspoon ground *cinnamon.* Set aside. Tear off four 9x18-inch pieces of heavy-duty foil. Fold each in half to make 4 squares. Fold up sides, forming pouches. Peel, halve, and pit 4 *peaches.* Place *two* peach halves in *each* pouch. Pour sherry mixture atop. Fold edges of foil to seal securely, leaving space for steam to build. Place beside the ribs. Grill directly over *medium-low* coals for 15 to 20 minutes or till heated through.

Tangy Spareribs

4 pounds meaty pork spareribs

● Cut ribs into serving-size pieces. Place in a Dutch oven. Add enough water to cover. Bring to boiling. Reduce heat. Simmer, covered, for 30 minutes. Drain.

½ cup chili sauce
⅓ cup chopped chutney
¼ cup steak sauce
2 tablespoons Worcestershire sauce

● Meanwhile, for sauce, in a small saucepan combine chili sauce, chutney, steak sauce, and Worcestershire sauce. In a covered grill arrange preheated coals around drip pan. Test for *slow* heat above pan. Pour 1 inch of water into pan. Place ribs on rack over pan. Lower hood. Grill about 45 minutes or till tender, brushing with sauce often. Heat and pass any remaining sauce. Serves 4.

Nutrition information per serving: 816 calories, 53 g protein, 27 g carbohydrate, 54 g fat, 214 mg cholesterol, 1,090 mg sodium, 851 mg potassium.

Make it easy. Simmer the ribs and prepare the sauce a day ahead. Then store them in the refrigerator until you're ready to grill.

Tex-Mex Smoked Short Ribs

4 **pounds beef short ribs** 4 **cups hickory wood chips**	● Place ribs in a Dutch oven. Add enough water to cover. Bring to boiling. Reduce heat. Simmer, covered, for 1½ hours. Drain ribs. At least 1 hour before cooking, soak wood chips in enough water to cover. Drain.
1½ **teaspoons chili powder** 1 **teaspoon dry mustard** ½ **teaspoon ground cumin** ⅛ **teaspoon garlic powder** 1 **tablespoon cooking oil** ½ **cup hot picante sauce** ¼ **teaspoon bottled hot pepper sauce**	● Meanwhile, for sauce, in a small saucepan cook chili powder, dry mustard, cumin, and garlic powder in cooking oil about 2 minutes or till the mixture sizzles. Remove from heat. Carefully stir in the picante sauce and hot pepper sauce.
	● In a covered grill arrange preheated coals around a drip pan. Test for *slow* heat above the pan. Pour 1 inch of water into the drip pan. Place drained wood chips on top of coals. Brush ribs with sauce. Place ribs on the grill rack over the drip pan but not over the coals. Lower grill hood. Grill for 20 to 30 minutes or till the ribs are tender, turning and brushing with sauce occasionally. Makes 6 servings.

Nutrition information per serving: 285 calories, 37 g protein, 1 g carbohydrate, 14 g fat, 113 mg cholesterol, 100 mg sodium, 312 mg potassium.

Forget neatness. These finger-lickin', tongue-ticklin' ribs are best eaten right off the bone.

Apricot Ribs

Pictured on the cover.

4 pounds pork loin back ribs *or* pork country-style ribs	● If desired, cut ribs into serving-size pieces. Place in a Dutch oven. Add enough water to cover. Bring to boiling. Reduce heat. Simmer, covered, for 30 minutes. Drain.
1 cup apricot preserves 2 tablespoons vinegar 1 tablespoon soy sauce ½ teaspoon grated gingerroot *or* ¼ teaspoon ground ginger 1 small fresh pineapple, cored and cut lengthwise into quarters	● For sauce, cook and stir preserves, vinegar, soy, and gingerroot till combined. In a covered grill arrange preheated coals around drip pan. Test for *slow* heat above pan. Pour 1 inch of water into pan. Place ribs on rack over pan. Lower hood. Grill for 30 minutes, brushing with sauce often. Place pineapple on grill. Brush with sauce. Grill 10 to 15 minutes more or till ribs are tender, brushing often with sauce. Pass any remaining sauce. Makes 4 servings.

Nutrition information per serving: 965 calories, 53 g protein, 67 g carbohydrate, 54 g fat, 214 mg cholesterol, 433 mg sodium, 750 mg potassium.

Cutting the pineapple quarters into chunks makes for easier eating. Use a long, thin-blade knife to cut between the pineapple and its rind. Then cut the wedges into 1-inch chunks. Replace the pineapple chunks atop the rind and grill as directed.

Coffee Ribs

4 cups hickory *or* other wood chips 4 pounds pork country-style ribs *or* pork loin back ribs	● One hour before cooking, soak chips in enough water to cover. Drain. Cut ribs into serving-size pieces. Place in a Dutch oven. Add enough water to cover. Bring to boiling. Reduce heat. Simmer, covered, for 30 minutes. Drain.
2 tablespoons brown sugar 2 teaspoons cornstarch 1½ teaspoons instant coffee crystals ½ teaspoon ground cinnamon ¼ teaspoon ground red pepper	● For glaze, in a small saucepan stir together brown sugar, cornstarch, coffee crystals, cinnamon, red pepper, and ½ teaspoon *salt.* Stir in 1 cup *water.* Cook and stir till thickened and bubbly. Cook and stir for 2 minutes more. In a covered grill arrange preheated coals around drip pan. Test for *slow* heat above pan. Pour 1 inch of water into pan. Place *1 cup* of chips on top of coals. Place ribs on rack over drip pan but not over coals. Brush ribs with glaze. Lower hood. Grill about 45 minutes or till tender, brushing with glaze occasionally. Add additional coals, chips, and water every 20 minutes or as necessary. Makes 4 servings.

Nutrition information per serving: 711 calories, 51 g protein, 2 g carbohydrate, 54 g fat, 214 mg cholesterol, 232 mg sodium, 576 mg potassium.

Our taste panelists loved the glaze on these ribs. But they couldn't decide whether to call it slightly sweet or slightly spicy. Give it a try and decide for yourself.

Apricot Ribs

Chicken Cranberry

2 to 2½ pounds meaty chicken pieces	● Rinse chicken, Pat dry with paper towels. If necessary, split breast pieces in half lengthwise. Sprinkle chicken pieces with salt and pepper.	**Why wait for Thanksgiving to enjoy cranberries? Chicken with cranberry sauce makes a great summertime treat.**

1 8-ounce can jellied cranberry sauce
¼ cup light corn syrup
2 tablespoons lemon juice
2 tablespoons margarine *or* butter, melted
½ teaspoon dried rosemary, crushed

● For sauce, in a mixing bowl stir together cranberry sauce, corn syrup, lemon juice, margarine or butter, and rosemary. Set aside.

● Grill chicken pieces, bone side up, on an uncovered grill directly over *medium* coals for 20 minutes. Turn chicken and grill for 20 to 30 minutes more or till tender, brushing often with the sauce during the last 15 minutes of cooking. Pass any remaining sauce. Makes 4 servings.

● **Microwave directions:** Arrange chicken, skin side up, in a 12x7½x2-inch microwave-safe baking dish with meatiest portions toward the outside of the dish. Cover loosely with waxed paper. Micro-cook on 100% power (high) for 8 to 10 minutes or till nearly tender, giving dish a half-turn after 5 minutes. Grill partially cooked chicken, bone side up, on an uncovered grill directly over *medium* coals for 10 to 15 minutes or till tender, turning once and brushing frequently with sauce. Serve chicken as above.

Nutrition information per serving: 351 calories, 23 g protein, 38 g carbohydrate, 12 g fat, 68 mg cholesterol, 166 mg sodium, 238 mg potassium.

Orange-Teriyaki Chicken

2 whole large chicken breasts (about 2 pounds total), halved lengthwise **⅓ cup teriyaki sauce** **⅓ cup frozen orange juice concentrate**	● Rinse chicken. Pat dry with paper towels. Place in a plastic bag set into a shallow dish. For marinade, combine teriyaki sauce and juice concentrate. Pour over chicken. Close bag. Marinate in the refrigerator for 6 to 24 hours, turning occasionally.	**Just two ingredients—teriyaki sauce and orange juice concentrate—combine in this Oriental-style marinade.**

● Drain chicken, reserving marinade. Grill chicken, bone side up, on an uncovered grill directly over *medium* coals for 20 minutes. Turn chicken and grill for 20 to 30 minutes more or till tender, brushing often with the reserved marinade. Makes 4 servings.

Nutrition information per serving: 200 calories, 36 g protein, 3 g carbohydrate, 4 g fat, 96 mg cholesterol, 314 mg sodium, 340 mg potassium.

Seeded Chicken Breasts

2 whole medium chicken breasts (about 1½ pounds total), skinned, halved lengthwise, and boned **2 tablespoons soy sauce** **½ teaspoon caraway seed** **½ teaspoon dill seed** **½ teaspoon celery seed**	● Rinse chicken pieces. Pat dry with paper towels. Rub soy sauce over the chicken breast halves. Crush caraway seed, dill seed, and celery seed. Place crushed seeds on a large piece of foil. Roll chicken in seeds. Wrap foil around chicken. Refrigerate for 2 to 24 hours.
Dairy sour cream *or* plain yogurt (optional)	● Remove chicken from the foil. Pat seeds onto the chicken breast halves. Grill on an uncovered grill directly over *medium* coals for 20 to 30 minutes or till tender, turning once. Serve with sour cream or plain yogurt, if desired. Makes 4 servings.

Nutrition information per serving: 149 calories, 27 g protein, 1 g carbohydrate, 3 g fat, 72 mg cholesterol, 578 mg sodium, 260 mg potassium.

Use your fingers to roll the chicken breast halves in the seed mixture. Then wrap the chicken portions in foil before chilling them. The chilling allows the flavors from the seeds to thoroughly blend, and the foil keeps the chicken from drying out.

Curried
Barbecued
Chicken

Curried Barbecued Chicken

1   2½- to 3-pound broiler-
    fryer chicken, cut into
    quarters
¼   cup cooking oil
½   teaspoon finely shredded
    lime peel
2   tablespoons lime juice
1   teaspoon curry powder
¼   teaspoon salt
¼   teaspoon ground cumin
¼   teaspoon ground coriander
1   clove garlic, minced

● Rinse chicken. Pat dry with paper towels. Break wing, hip, and drumstick joints of chicken so quarters will lie flat. Twist wing tips under back.

For marinade, stir together cooking oil, lime peel, lime juice, curry, salt, cumin, coriander, minced garlic, and ⅛ teaspoon *pepper*. Place chicken in a plastic bag set into a shallow dish. Pour marinade over chicken. Close the bag. Marinate in the refrigerator for 6 to 24 hours, turning occasionally.

● Drain chicken, reserving marinade. Grill chicken, bone side up, on an uncovered grill directly over *medium* coals for 20 minutes. Turn chicken and grill for 20 to 30 minutes more or till tender, brushing frequently with the reserved marinade. Makes 4 servings.

Nutrition information per serving: 214 calories, 27 g protein, 0 g carbohydrate, 11 g fat, 82 mg cholesterol, 116 mg sodium, 257 mg potassium.

Serving Suggestion:
Lemon Vegetables
Tear off an 18x36-inch piece of heavy-duty foil. Fold in half to make a square. Fold up sides to form a pouch. In pouch place 2 cups frozen mixed *broccoli, French-style green beans, onions, and red pepper,* 2 tablespoons *water,* 2 tablespoons *margarine,* ½ teaspoon finely shredded *lemon peel,* and ⅛ teaspoon *lemon-pepper seasoning.* Seal edges, leaving space for steam to build. Place on grill next to chicken. Grill for 25 to 30 minutes or till crisp-tender, turning occasionally.

Plum-Good Chicken

2   to 2½ pounds meaty
    chicken pieces

● Rinse chicken. Pat dry with paper towels. Sprinkle with salt and pepper.

½   cup plum jam
2   tablespoons lemon juice
2   tablespoons water
¼   teaspoon ground ginger
¼   teaspoon onion powder

● For sauce, in a saucepan combine plum jam, lemon juice, water, ground ginger, and onion powder. Cook and stir till jam melts.

● Grill chicken pieces, bone side up, on an uncovered grill directly over *medium* coals for 20 minutes. Turn chicken and grill for 20 to 30 minutes more or till tender. Brush often with sauce during the last 15 minutes of cooking. Drizzle any remaining sauce on chicken before serving. Makes 4 to 6 servings.

Nutrition information per serving: 294 calories, 29 g protein, 27 g carbohydrate, 8 g fat, 85 mg cholesterol, 89 mg sodium, 303 mg potassium.

If plum jam isn't available at your grocery, substitute apricot jam.

Saucy Chicken Legs

8 **chicken drumsticks**
1 **teaspoon dried minced onion**
¼ **cup catsup**
1 **tablespoon steak sauce**

● Rinse chicken drumsticks. Pat dry with paper towels. For sauce, stir together dried onion and 2 tablespoons *water*. Let stand for 5 minutes. Stir in catsup and steak sauce.

● Grill chicken on an uncovered grill directly over *medium* coals for 35 to 45 minutes or till tender, turning once. Brush with the sauce during the last 10 minutes of cooking. Makes 4 servings.

● **Microwave directions:** Rinse chicken and prepare sauce as above. In a 12x7½x2-inch microwave-safe baking dish arrange chicken with meatiest portions toward outside of dish. Cover loosely with waxed paper. Micro-cook on 100% power (high) for 8 minutes, giving dish a half-turn after 4 minutes. Grill partially-cooked chicken on an uncovered grill directly over *medium* coals for 10 to 15 minutes or till tender, turning once and brushing often with sauce.

Nutrition information per serving: 176 calories, 25 g protein, 6 g carbohydrate, 5 g fat, 82 mg cholesterol, 347 mg sodium, 309 mg potassium.

If rain is threatening, cut the grilling time by starting the drumsticks in the microwave.

Lemon Turkey

2 **turkey breast tenderloin steaks**
¼ **cup cooking oil**
2 **tablespoons lemon juice**
2 **tablespoons water**
1 **teaspoon sugar**
1 **teaspoon dried sage, crushed**
1 **clove garlic, minced**

● Rinse turkey steaks. Pat dry with paper towels. Place in a plastic bag set into a shallow dish. For marinade, stir together cooking oil, lemon juice, water, sugar, sage, garlic, ¼ teaspoon *salt*, and ⅛ teaspoon *pepper*. Pour over turkey in the bag. Close bag. Marinate in the refrigerator for 6 to 24 hours, turning the bag occasionally.

● Drain turkey, reserving marinade. Grill on an uncovered grill directly over *medium* coals for 12 to 14 minutes or till tender, turning once and brushing often with reserved marinade. Serves 2.

Nutrition information per serving: 217 calories, 34 g protein, 1 g carbohydrate, 8 g fat, 94 mg cholesterol, 125 mg sodium, 339 mg potassium.

The refreshing lemon marinade was a hit with our taste panel.

Peach-Sauced Cornish Hens

2 1- to 1½-pound Cornish game hens, halved lengthwise

● Rinse Cornish hens. Pat dry with paper towels. Break wing and drumstick joints so halves will lie flat during cooking. Twist wing tips under backs.

1 4½-ounce jar strained peaches (baby food)
¼ cup orange juice
¼ teaspoon ground nutmeg

● For sauce, combine peaches, orange juice, and nutmeg. Set aside. Grill Cornish game hen halves, bone side up, on an uncovered grill directly over *medium* coals for 20 minutes. Turn hens and grill for 20 to 25 minutes more or till tender. Brush often with sauce during the last 15 minutes of cooking. Heat any remaining sauce and pass with the hens. Makes 4 servings.

Nutrition information per serving: 172 calories, 22 g protein, 8 g carbohydrate, 6 g fat, 64 mg cholesterol, 66 mg sodium, 277 mg potassium.

Using baby-food strained peaches may sound strange, but it spares you the mess and fuss of pureeing your own fruit.

Herbed Turkey

4 turkey breast tenderloin steaks (1 to 1¼ pounds total)
½ cup white grape juice
¼ cup cooking oil
2 tablespoons vinegar
2 tablespoons sliced green onion
¼ teaspoon celery salt
¼ teaspoon dried thyme, crushed
⅛ teaspoon dried rosemary, crushed

● Rinse turkey. Pat dry with paper towels. Place turkey in a plastic bag set into a shallow dish. For marinade, combine grape juice, oil, vinegar, onion, celery salt, thyme, and rosemary. Pour marinade over turkey in bag. Close bag. Marinate in the refrigerator for 6 to 24 hours, turning the bag several times.

● Drain turkey, reserving marinade. Grill on an uncovered grill directly over *medium* coals for 12 to 14 minutes or till tender, turning once and brushing often with reserved marinade. Serves 4.

Nutrition information per serving: 189 calories, 34 g protein, 1 g carbohydrate, 4 g fat, 94 mg cholesterol, 87 mg sodium, 344 mg potassium.

Serving Suggestion:
Cheese Bread
    Bake one 5- to 8-ounce loaf of *brown-and-serve French bread* according to package directions. Cut the bread into 8 slices, cutting to, but not through, the bottom crust. Stir together ¼ cup shredded *cheddar cheese*, 1 tablespoon softened *margarine* or *butter*, ¼ teaspoon *dry mustard*, and dash *pepper*. Spread between the bread slices. Wrap loosely in heavy-duty foil. Place on the grill rack beside the turkey. Grill over coals for 8 to 10 minutes or till cheese melts, turning frequently.

Italian-Style Chicken Quarters

1 2½- to 3-pound broiler-fryer chicken, cut into quarters	● Rinse chicken quarters. Pat dry with paper towels. Break wing, hip, and drumstick joints of the chicken so quarters will lie flat during cooking. Twist wing tips under back.
1 8-ounce can tomato sauce **2 tablespoons clear Italian salad dressing** **1 tablespoon dried parsley flakes** **1 teaspoon Worcestershire sauce**	● For sauce, in a bowl combine tomato sauce, salad dressing, parsley flakes, and Worcestershire sauce; set aside.
	● Grill chicken quarters, bone side up, on an uncovered grill directly over *medium-hot* coals for 20 minutes. Turn chicken and grill for 20 to 30 minutes more or till tender, brushing often with the sauce during the last 15 minutes of grilling. Heat any remaining sauce and pass with chicken. Makes 4 servings.
	● **Microwave directions:** Arrange chicken, skin side up, in a 12x7½x2-inch microwave-safe baking dish with meatiest portions toward the outside of the dish. Cover loosely with waxed paper. Micro-cook on 100% power (high) about 10 minutes or till nearly tender, giving dish a half-turn after 5 minutes. Grill partially cooked chicken, bone side up, on an uncovered grill directly over *medium* coals for 10 to 15 minutes or till tender, brushing frequently with sauce. Serve chicken as above.

Getting chicken quarters to lie flat on the grill is easy. Just apply pressure to the wing, hip, and drumstick joints, then twist the limbs.

Nutrition information per serving: 236 calories, 28 g protein, 5 g carbohydrate, 11 g fat, 82 mg cholesterol, 499 mg sodium, 471 mg potassium.

Mint Chicken Breasts

Mint Chicken Breasts

2 whole medium chicken breasts (1½ pounds total)
½ cup dry white wine
1 tablespoon snipped fresh mint
1 tablespoon margarine
¼ teaspoon crushed red pepper
½ cup dairy sour cream (optional)

Mint leaves (optional)

● Halve chicken breasts lengthwise. Rinse chicken. Pat dry with paper towels. For glaze, in a small saucepan combine wine, mint, margarine, and red pepper. Cook and stir till margarine melts. If sour cream sauce is desired, stir *2 tablespoons* of the glaze into the sour cream. Chill till serving time.

● Grill chicken, bone side up, on an uncovered grill directly over *medium* coals for 20 minutes. Turn and grill 15 to 25 minutes more or till tender, brushing often with glaze. Pass sour cream sauce and garnish with mint leaves, if desired. Makes 4 servings.

Nutrition information per serving: 194 calories, 35 g protein, 10 g carbohydrate, 1 g fat, 94 mg cholesterol, 412 mg sodium, 507 mg potassium.

The long, hot days of summer call for the light, refreshing taste of mint.

Orange-Sauced Turkey Tenderloin

4 turkey breast tenderloin steaks
1 teaspoon finely shredded orange peel
¼ cup orange juice
2 tablespoons molasses
1 tablespoon catsup
1 tablespoon prepared mustard
1 tablespoon soy sauce
¼ teaspoon garlic powder
Dash bottled hot pepper sauce

● Rinse turkey. Pat dry with paper towels. For sauce, in a mixing bowl stir together orange peel, orange juice, molasses, catsup, mustard, soy sauce, garlic powder, and hot pepper sauce. Grill turkey tenderloin steaks on an uncovered grill directly over *medium* coals for 12 to 14 minutes, turning once and brushing often with sauce. Pass any remaining sauce. Makes 4 servings.

Nutrition information per serving: 191 calories, 26 g protein, 1 g carbohydrate, 6 g fat, 72 mg cholesterol, 98 mg sodium, 254 mg potassium.

For hearty turkey sandwiches, serve these tenderloin steaks on toasted kaiser rolls with extra sauce.

Lamb Rib Roast With Mint

Cutting slits in the roast before marinating it helps the flavors penetrate to the center of the meat.

½ cup mint jelly
½ cup white wine vinegar
2 tablespoons cooking oil
1 tablespoon grated onion
¼ teaspoon pepper

● For marinade, in a small saucepan combine jelly, vinegar, cooking oil, grated onion, and pepper. Cook and stir over low heat till jelly melts. Set aside.

1 1½- to 1¾-pound lamb rib roast (8 to 10 ribs)

● Trim any excess fat from roast. On top side of roast, cut slits 1½ inches apart and ½ inch deep. Place roast in a plastic bag set into a shallow dish. Pour marinade over meat. Close bag and marinate in the refrigerator for 6 to 24 hours, turning the bag several times.

● Drain meat, reserving the marinade. Use paper towels to pat the meat dry. Insert a meat thermometer near the center of the roast, not touching the bones. In a covered grill arrange preheated coals around a drip pan. Test for *medium* heat above the pan. Pour 1 inch of water into the drip pan. Place roast, bone side down, on the grill rack over the drip pan but not over coals. Lower grill hood. Grill to desired doneness, brushing occasionally with reserved marinade during last 15 minutes of cooking. (Allow 50 to 55 minutes for 140° [rare], 55 to 60 minutes for 160° [medium], and 60 to 65 minutes for 170° [well-done].) Serves 3 or 4.

Nutrition information per serving: 237 calories, 23 g protein, 10 g carbohydrate, 11 g fat, 86 mg cholesterol, 59 mg sodium, 282 mg potassium.

Lemon-Curried Chuck Roast

1 **2- to 3-pound beef chuck arm pot roast, cut 1½ inches thick**	● Slash fat edges of roast at 1-inch intervals, being careful not to cut into the meat. Place roast in a plastic bag set into a shallow dish.
⅓ **cup soy sauce** ⅓ **cup lemon juice** 1 **tablespoon sugar** 1 **tablespoon grated onion** 1 **tablespoon cooking oil** 1 **teaspoon curry powder** 1 **teaspoon chili powder**	● For marinade, in a bowl combine soy sauce, lemon juice, sugar, onion, cooking oil, curry powder, and chili powder. Pour marinade over meat. Close bag and marinate in the refrigerator for 6 to 24 hours, turning occasionally.

● Drain roast, reserving marinade. In a covered grill arrange preheated coals around a drip pan. Test for *medium* heat above the pan. Pour 1 inch of water into the drip pan. Place roast on the grill rack over the drip pan but not over the coals. Lower grill hood. Grill to desired doneness, brushing occasionally with the reserved marinade. (Allow 40 to 45 minutes for 140° [rare], 45 to 50 minutes for 160° [medium], and 50 to 55 minutes for 170° [well-done].) Add additional coals and water every 20 to 30 minutes or as necessary. Makes 8 servings.

Nutrition information per serving: 186 calories, 25 g protein, 1 g carbohydrate, 8 g fat, 77 mg cholesterol, 224 mg sodium, 236 mg potassium.

Grilling isn't just for expensive cuts of meat. This recipe makes a juicy meal of a less-tender beef roast by cooking it slowly over indirect heat.

Herbed Rib Roast with Dijon-Sour-Cream Sauce

¾ **cup dry red wine**
½ **cup finely chopped onion**
¼ **cup lemon juice**
¼ **cup water**
1 **tablespoon Worcestershire sauce**
½ **teaspoon dried rosemary, crushed**
½ **teaspoon dried marjoram, crushed**
¼ **teaspoon garlic salt**
1 **4-pound beef rib roast**

● For marinade, in a mixing bowl combine wine, onion, lemon juice, water, Worcestershire sauce, rosemary, marjoram, and garlic salt. Place beef roast in a large plastic bag set into a shallow dish. Pour marinade over meat. Close bag. Marinate in the refrigerator for 6 to 24 hours, turning occasionally. Drain meat, reserving marinade. Insert a meat thermometer into the center of the roast, not touching the bones.

A beef rib roast is easily identified by the solid round of meat (the rib eye muscle) in the center of the roast. When shopping for the roast, you also may see it labeled beef standing rib roast or beef prime rib.

4 **mesquite wood chunks or 4 cups mesquite wood chips**

● At least 1 hour before cooking, soak wood chunks or chips in enough water to cover. Drain wood chunks or chips. In a covered grill arrange preheated coals around a drip pan. Test for *medium* heat above the pan. Pour 1 inch of water into the drip pan. Place all of the drained wood chunks or *1 cup* of the drained wood chips on top of the preheated coals. Place roast, fat side up, on the grill rack over the drip pan but not over the coals. Lower grill hood. Grill to desired doneness, brushing with reserved marinade every 20 to 30 minutes. (Allow 2¼ to 2¾ hours for 140° [rare], 2¾ to 3¼ hours for 160° [medium], and 3¼ to 3¾ hours for 170° [well-done].) Add additional coals, wood chips, and water every 20 to 30 minutes or as necessary.

1 **8-ounce carton dairy sour cream**
2 **tablespoons Dijon-style mustard**
½ **teaspoon lemon-pepper seasoning**

● Meanwhile, for sauce, stir together sour cream, Dijon-style mustard, and lemon-pepper seasoning. Cover and chill till serving time. Slice roast to serve. Dollop with sauce. Makes 8 servings.

Nutrition information per serving: 299 calories, 24 g protein, 2 g carbohydrate, 20 g fat, 90 mg cholesterol, 250 mg sodium, 404 mg potassium.

Barbecued Beef Brisket

1 3- to 4-pound fresh beef
  brisket
½ cup water
½ cup homemade barbecue
  sauce (see recipes,
  pages 20–23) *or* bottled
  barbecue sauce
1 small onion, finely
  chopped
2 tablespoons
  Worcestershire sauce
1 tablespoon instant coffee
  crystals
1 tablespoon vinegar
1 tablespoon cooking oil
3 cloves garlic, minced
½ teaspoon seasoned pepper

● Place brisket in a plastic bag set into a shallow dish. For marinade, in a bowl combine water, barbecue sauce, onion, Worcestershire sauce, coffee crystals, vinegar, cooking oil, garlic, and pepper. Pour marinade over meat in the bag. Close the bag and marinate in the refrigerator for 6 to 24 hours, turning the bag occasionally.

● Drain meat, reserving the marinade. In a covered grill arrange preheated coals around a drip pan. Test for *slow* heat above the pan. Pour 1 inch of water into the drip pan. Place brisket, fat side up, on the grill rack over the drip pan but not over the coals. Brush with reserved marinade. Lower grill hood. Grill for 2 to 2½ hours or till tender, brushing with reserved marinade every 20 to 30 minutes. Add additional coals and water every 20 to 30 minutes or as necessary. To serve, thinly slice the brisket across the grain. Heat any remaining marinade and pass with meat. Serves 12.

Nutrition information per serving: 194 calories, 21 g protein, 2 g carbohydrate, 10 g fat, 66 mg cholesterol, 166 mg sodium, 239 mg potassium.

Coffee crystals add a flavor twist to traditional barbecue-sauced brisket.

Smoked Rhubarb-Glazed Pork Roast

4 cups applewood *or* cherry wood chips
1 2-pound pork loin roast with backbone loosened

● At least 1 hour before cooking, soak wood chips in enough water to cover. Drain chips. In a covered grill arrange preheated coals around a drip pan. Test for *medium* heat above pan. Place *1 cup* of the drained wood chips on top of preheated coals. Insert a meat thermometer into the center of the roast. Place roast on grill rack over the drip pan but not over the coals. Lower grill hood. Grill for 1 hour. Add additional coals, wood chips, and water every 20 to 30 minutes or as necessary.

Rhubarb from your backyard makes a terrific glaze. But if you don't have a fresh supply, a package of frozen rhubarb from the grocery works just as well.

¾ pound fresh *or* frozen rhubarb, sliced (2¼ cups)
1 6-ounce can apple juice concentrate
Few drops red food coloring (optional)
2 tablespoons honey
Lettuce leaves (optional)
Red seedless grapes (optional)

● Meanwhile, prepare rhubarb glaze. In a saucepan combine rhubarb, juice concentrate, and, if desired, red food coloring. Bring to boiling. Reduce heat. Cover and simmer for 15 to 20 minutes or till rhubarb is very tender. Strain, pressing liquid out of pulp. Discard pulp. Return liquid to the saucepan. Bring to a boil. Simmer, uncovered, for 10 to 15 minutes or till rhubarb liquid is reduced to ½ cup. Stir in honey. Brush glaze on meat. Grill, covered, for 45 to 60 minutes more or till meat thermometer registers 170°, brushing twice with glaze. Line serving platter with lettuce, if desired. Transfer meat to platter; garnish with grapes, if desired. Slice to serve. Makes 4 to 6 servings.

Nutrition information per serving: 385 calories, 29 g protein, 34 g carbohydrate, 15 g fat, 93 mg cholesterol, 88 mg sodium, 867 mg potassium.

Apple-Corn-Bread-Stuffed Chicken

½ cup thinly sliced celery
¼ cup sliced green onion
¼ cup margarine *or* butter
2 cups corn bread stuffing mix
1 large apple, peeled, cored, and finely chopped (about 1¼ cups)
1 cup soft bread cubes
½ cup shredded cheddar cheese (2 ounces)
⅓ to ½ cup water

● For stuffing, in a saucepan cook celery and onion in margarine or butter till tender. In a mixing bowl combine corn bread stuffing mix, apple, bread cubes, cheese, and celery mixture. Toss with enough water to moisten. Set aside.

1 3½- to 4½-pound whole roasting chicken

● Rinse chicken; pat dry. Sprinkle insides of cavities with salt. Spoon some of the stuffing into the neck cavity. Skewer neck skin to back. Lightly spoon stuffing into the body cavity; *do not pack.* Tie legs to tail. Twist wing tips under back. Tear off an 18x24-inch piece of heavy-duty foil. Fold in half to make a double thickness of foil that measures 12x18 inches. Place remaining stuffing in the center of foil. Bring up long edges of foil and seal with a double fold. Then fold short ends to completely encase the packet, leaving space for steam to build. Refrigerate the packet till ready to grill.

Cooking oil
¼ cup currant jelly
2 teaspoons prepared mustard

● In a covered grill arrange preheated coals around a drip pan. Test for *medium* heat above the pan. Pour 1 inch of water into the drip pan. Place the stuffed bird, breast side up, on the grill rack over the drip pan but not over coals. Brush bird with cooking oil. Insert a meat thermometer into center of inside thigh muscle, not touching bone. Lower grill hood. Grill for 1 to 1¼ hours or till meat thermometer registers 180° to 185°. Add additional coals and water every 20 to 30 minutes or as necessary. Place foil packet of stuffing on grill rack beside chicken during last 20 minutes of grilling.

Meanwhile, in a small saucepan cook and stir the jelly till melted. Stir in the mustard. Brush on bird during the last 15 minutes of cooking. Makes 6 servings.

Nutrition information per serving: 536 calories, 34 g protein, 51 g carbohydrate, 22 g fat, 88 mg cholesterol, 934 mg sodium, 386 mg potassium.

Serving Suggestion:
Sherried Mushrooms
Tear off an 18x36-inch piece of heavy-duty foil. Fold in half to make a square. Fold up sides, using your fist to make a pouch. In the pouch place ½ pound fresh whole *mushrooms,* 2 tablespoons *margarine* or *butter,* 1 tablespoon *dry sherry,* and ½ teaspoon crushed, dried *marjoram.* Fold edges to seal pouch securely, leaving space for steam to build. Place beside chicken on the grill rack. Grill directly over *medium-hot* coals about 20 minutes or till tender.

Peppery Smoked Chicken

4 cups hickory wood chips *or* 4 to 6 mesquite wood chunks	● At least 1 hour before cooking, soak wood chips or chunks in enough water to cover. Drain.

2 tablespoons brandy
2 teaspoons cracked black peppercorns
1 teaspoon cooking oil
1 to 2 cloves garlic, minced
½ teaspoon salt
1 2½- to 3-pound broiler-fryer chicken

● Meanwhile, stir together brandy, peppercorns, oil, garlic, and salt. Rinse chicken. Pat dry. Skewer neck skin to back. Tie legs to tail. Twist wing tips under back. Brush chicken with pepper mixture. In covered grill arrange preheated coals around drip pan. Test for *medium* heat above pan. Pour 1 inch of water into pan. Place *1 cup* of wood chips (or all of the wood chunks) on top of preheated coals. Place chicken, breast side up, on grill rack over pan. Lower hood. Grill about 1 hour or till a drumstick moves easily in its socket. Add additional coals, wood chips, and water every 20 to 30 minutes or as necessary. Makes 6 servings.

Nutrition information per serving: 141 calories, 18 g protein, 0 g carbohydrate, 6 g fat, 55 mg cholesterol, 233 mg sodium, 172 mg potassium.

We stole the traditional seasonings from steak au poivre—pepper and brandy—and added them to smoked chicken, creating a sensational flavor combination.

Smokers

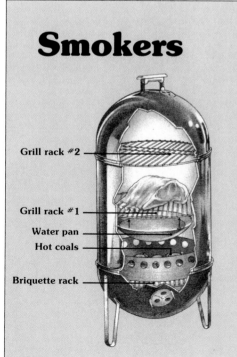

Grill rack #2
Grill rack #1
Water pan
Hot coals
Briquette rack

Water smokers are unique grills designed for smoke-cooking. Their shape allows slightly better circulation of heat and steam around the food than in regular covered grills. A popular style is the charcoal dome, shown at left. Smokers also can be heated by gas or electricity. Be sure to read the manufacturer's instructions for proper use. Although all charcoal domes are not exactly alike, the basic procedure is the same. Once the coals are heated, place the wet wood chunks atop. Then place the meat on the grill rack. Keep the food moist while it cooks by filling the water pan with water, wine, or fruit juice. After a couple of hours, check to see if you need to add more charcoal, wood chunks, or liquid.

Five-Spice Smoked Turkey Breast

4 cups applewood *or* Osage orangewood chips	● At least 1 hour before cooking, soak wood chips in enough water to cover. Drain wood chips.

1 teaspoon ground cinnamon 1 teaspoon aniseed, crushed, *or* 1 star anise, crushed ½ teaspoon salt ¼ teaspoon fennel seed, crushed ¼ teaspoon coarse ground pepper *or* Szechwan pepper ⅛ teaspoon ground cloves 1 2- to 3-pound turkey breast portion Cooking oil	● For the seasoning mixture, stir together ground cinnamon, aniseed or anise, salt, fennel seed, pepper or Szechwan pepper, and cloves. Remove skin from the turkey breast; discard. Rinse turkey. Pat dry with paper towels. Brush the turkey breast with cooking oil. Rub the seasoning mixture onto the turkey breast.

● In a covered grill arrange preheated coals around a drip pan. Test for *medium* heat above the pan. Place *1 cup* of the drained wood chips on top of the preheated coals. Insert a meat thermometer into the turkey breast. Place the turkey breast on the grill rack over the drip pan but not over the coals. Lower the grill hood. Grill for 1 to 1½ hours or till thermometer registers 170°. (The seasoning mixture will cause the outside of the turkey breast to appear dark.) Add additional coals and wood chips every 20 to 30 minutes or as necessary. Makes 4 to 6 servings.

Nutrition information per serving: 216 calories, 41 g protein, 1 g carbohydrate, 5 g fat, 112 mg cholesterol, 337 mg sodium, 408 mg potassium.

For a quick seasoning mixture, stir together 2½ teaspoons purchased *five-spice powder* and ½ teaspoon *salt.* Use the mixture in place of all the other seasonings.

Grilled Turkey With Peanut Dressing

1 9- to 11-pound turkey
Cooking oil

● Rinse turkey. Pat dry with paper towels. Sprinkle insides of cavities with salt. Skewer neck skin to back. Tie legs to the tail. Twist wing tips under back. Insert a meat thermometer into the center of the inside thigh muscle, not touching the bone. In a covered grill arrange preheated coals around a large drip pan. Test for *medium* heat above the pan. Pour 1 inch of water into the drip pan. Place unstuffed bird, breast side up, on the grill rack over the drip pan but not over the coals. Brush the bird with cooking oil. Lower grill hood. Grill for 2½ to 3 hours or till meat thermometer registers 180° to 185°, brushing occasionally with cooking oil. Add additional coals and water every 20 to 30 minutes or as necessary.

---

  1 **cup finely chopped celery**
  ½ **cup chopped onion**
1½ **teaspoons ground sage**
  ⅔ **cup margarine *or* butter**
1¼ **cups salted peanuts, chopped**
  ⅓ **cup snipped parsley**
  ½ **teaspoon pepper**
  8 **cups dry bread cubes (11 to 12 slices)**
  ¾ **to 1 cup water**

● Meanwhile, prepare dressing. In a saucepan cook celery, onion, and sage in margarine or butter till tender. Stir in peanuts, parsley, and pepper. In a large mixing bowl combine bread cubes and peanut mixture. Toss with enough water to moisten. Tear off an 18x48-inch piece of heavy-duty foil. Fold in half to make a double thickness of foil that measures 18x24-inches. Place peanut mixture in the center of the foil. Bring up long edges of foil and seal with a double fold. Then fold short ends to completely encase the packet, leaving space for steam to build. Place foil packet beside the turkey during the last 25 to 30 minutes of cooking or till heated through.

  Cover bird with foil and let stand 15 minutes before carving. Serve dressing with turkey. Makes 12 servings.

Nutrition information per serving: 620 calories, 72 g protein, 23 g carbohydrate, 26 g fat, 214 mg cholesterol, 530 mg sodium, 770 mg potassium.

Use your microwave to reduce cooking time. Prepare turkey as directed. Cover wing tips and legs with small pieces of foil. Place, breast side down, on rack in a microwave-safe baking dish. Brush with cooking oil. Cover with waxed paper. Micro-cook on 100% power (high) 3 minutes per pound, giving a half-turn once. Turn breast side up; brush with cooking oil. Cook, covered, on high 1½ minutes per pound, giving a half-turn once. Insert a microwave meat thermometer into thigh muscle. Cook, covered, on high 1½ minutes per pound or till thermometer registers 140°, giving dish a half-turn once. Remove thermometer. Brush turkey with cooking oil.

  Meanwhile, prepare grill and stuffing as directed. Test for *medium* heat above pan. Place turkey, breast side up, on rack over drip pan but not over coals. Insert a conventional meat thermometer. Lower hood. Grill for 50 to 60 minutes or till thermometer registers 180° to 185°, brushing occasionally with cooking oil.

Fish and Squash on a Skewer

1 **pound swordfish, sea bass, shark,** *or* **tuna steaks, cut 1 inch thick**	● Remove skin and bones from fish, if necessary. Cut fish into 1-inch pieces. Place in a plastic bag set into a bowl.
1 **teaspoon finely shredded lime peel** 3 **tablespoons lime juice** 3 **tablespoons cooking oil** 2 **teaspoons sesame oil**	● For marinade, in a mixing bowl combine lime peel, lime juice, cooking oil, and sesame oil. Pour marinade over the fish in the bag. Close bag and marinate in the refrigerator for 1 to 4 hours, turning occasionally.
2 **small yellow summer squash** 8 **green onions, cut into 1½-inch pieces** **Cooking oil** 1 **tablespoon snipped parsley**	● Cut the squash into 1-inch slices. In a saucepan precook the squash, covered, in a small amount of boiling water for 2 minutes. Drain. Drain fish, reserving the marinade. On 5 long skewers, alternately thread fish, squash, and green onions, leaving about ¼ inch between foods. Brush cooking oil on the grill rack. Grill on an uncovered grill directly over *medium-hot* coals for 8 to 10 minutes or till fish flakes easily, turning often and brushing frequently with reserved marinade. Sprinkle with parsley before serving. Makes 5 servings.

Nutrition information per serving: 192 calories, 18 g protein, 5 g carbohydrate, 11 g fat, 50 mg cholesterol, 51 mg sodium, 570 mg potassium.

To avoid having your fish fall off during grilling, we suggest you make your kabobs with a firm-fleshed fish such as swordfish, sea bass, shark, or tuna.

Beef 'n' Beer Kabobs

1 **pound boneless beef sirloin steak, cut 1 inch thick**	● Cut steak into 1-inch cubes. Place in a plastic bag set into a bowl. For marinade, stir together beer, chopped onion, cooking oil, fresh or dried oregano, salt, and garlic powder. Pour over meat. Close bag. Marinate in the refrigerator for 6 to 24 hours, turning occasionally.	**Beer makes an easy and delicious base for a marinade.**

1 **pound boneless beef sirloin steak, cut 1 inch thick**
½ **of a 12-ounce can (¾ cup) beer**
1 **small onion, finely chopped**
2 **tablespoons cooking oil**
1 **tablespoon snipped fresh oregano** *or* **1 teaspoon dried oregano, crushed**
¼ **teaspoon salt**
⅛ **teaspoon garlic powder**

2 **medium green** *or* **red sweet peppers**
8 **ounces whole fresh mushrooms**

● Cut peppers into 1-inch squares. In a large saucepan precook the pepper squares and mushrooms, covered, in a small amount of boiling water for 2 minutes. Drain. Drain meat cubes, reserving marinade.

● On 4 long or 8 short skewers, alternately thread beef cubes, pepper squares, and mushrooms, leaving about ¼ inch between foods. Grill on an uncovered grill directly over *medium-hot* coals for 6 to 8 minutes or to desired doneness, turning often and brushing frequently with reserved marinade. Makes 4 servings.

Nutrition information per serving: 203 calories, 23 g protein, 6 g carbohydrate, 9 g fat, 56 mg cholesterol, 88 mg sodium, 628 mg potassium.

Surf and Turf Kabobs

8 ounces fresh *or* frozen shelled large shrimp ¾ pound boneless beef sirloin steak 2 small summer squash *or* zucchini, *or* 1 of each 2 small onions, quartered	● Thaw shrimp, if frozen. Set aside. Cut meat into 1-inch pieces. Diagonally cut summer squash or zucchini into 1-inch slices. In a saucepan cook squash and onions in a small amount of boiling water about 1 minute or till almost tender. Drain.
¼ cup lemon juice 2 tablespoons cooking oil ½ teaspoon dried dillweed ¼ teaspoon salt ¼ teaspoon paprika	● For sauce, combine lemon juice, oil, dillweed, salt, and paprika. On 4 long skewers, alternately thread shrimp, beef, squash, and onion, leaving about ¼ inch space between foods. Brush with sauce.
Cherry tomatoes	● Grill on an uncovered grill directly over *medium-hot* coals for 10 to 12 minutes or till done, turning and brushing with sauce often. Garnish with tomatoes. Makes 4 servings.

Nutrition information per serving: 213 calories, 28 g protein, 6 g carbohydrate, 8 g fat, 128 mg cholesterol, 158 mg sodium, 528 mg potassium.

Surf's up! Serve these beef and shrimp kabobs at your next beach party. Or, if you don't have a beach handy, decorate your backyard to look like one and serve the kabobs at home. Use beach towels for tablecloths and play volleyball using a beach ball.

Turkey Kabobs

2 large sweet potatoes (about 8 ounces each)	● Cut off woody portions of potatoes. Cook potatoes, covered, in enough boiling salted water to cover for 30 to 35 minutes or till almost tender. Drain and cool. Peel. Cut into 1-inch pieces.
1¼ pounds turkey breast tenderloin 1 2½- or 3-ounce package thinly sliced smoked ham, halved 2 tablespoons cooking oil 2 tablespoons corn syrup 1 tablespoon lemon juice ¾ teaspoon caraway seed ¼ teaspoon onion powder	● Meanwhile, cut turkey into 1-inch pieces. Fold ham pieces to make narrow strips. Wrap a ham strip around each turkey piece. On 4 long skewers, alternately thread ham-wrapped turkey pieces and potato pieces, leaving about ¼ inch space between foods. For sauce, in a small bowl stir together cooking oil, corn syrup, lemon juice, caraway seed, and onion powder.
	● Brush sauce over kabobs. Grill on an uncovered grill directly over *medium-hot* coals for 10 to 15 minutes or till turkey is tender, turning and brushing with sauce frequently. Makes 4 servings.

Nutrition information per serving: 394 calories, 38 g protein, 37 g carbohydrate, 10 g fat, 101 mg cholesterol, 357 mg sodium, 625 mg potassium.

Leaving a small space between the foods on the skewer allows for more even cooking.

Surf and Turf Kabobs

Wild-Rice-Stuffed Salmon

2 cups hickory wood chips
1 cup wild rice
2 cups chicken broth
½ cup shredded carrot
¼ cup sliced green onion
1 tablespoon margarine *or* butter
1 3- to 4-pound whole dressed salmon, head removed

● At least 1 hour before cooking, soak wood chips in enough water to cover. Drain chips. Run cold water over rice in a strainer about 1 minute, lifting rice to rinse well. In a saucepan combine rice, chicken broth, carrot, green onion, and margarine or butter. Bring to boiling. Reduce heat. Simmer, covered, 40 to 50 minutes or till liquid is absorbed. Sprinkle fish cavity with salt and pepper.

● Spoon *½ cups* of the rice mixture into the cavity of the salmon. Skewer or tie the salmon closed. Tear off an 18x36-inch piece of heavy-duty foil. Fold in half to make a square. Fold up sides to form a pouch. Place the remaining rice mixture in the pouch. Seal edges, leaving space for steam to build. Refrigerate the pouch till ready to grill.

In a covered grill arrange preheated coals around a drip pan. Test for *medium* heat above the pan. Place *1 cup* of the drained wood chips on top of the preheated coals. Tear off a piece of heavy-duty foil large enough to hold the salmon. Prick several holes in the foil. Place on the grill rack over the drip pan but not over the coals. Place fish on foil. Lower grill hood. Grill for 40 to 50 minutes or till fish flakes easily with a fork. Place foil packet of rice beside fish on the grill rack during the last 15 minutes of cooking. Add additional wood chips every 20 to 30 minutes or as necessary. Makes 6 servings.

Nutrition information per serving: 320 calories, 30 g protein, 22 g carbohydrate, 12 g fat, 70 mg cholesterol, 361 mg sodium, 609 mg potassium.

Fresh salmon and wild rice make this recipe a bit expensive, but our taste panel thought the flavor was worth the cost.

Use a spoon to lightly place some of the rice stuffing in the salmon. The remaining stuffing is cooked separately in a foil packet on the grill.

Lobster Tails Elegante

4 frozen lobster tails (7 to 8 ounces each)	● Thaw lobster tails. To butterfly tails, cut lengthwise through centers of hard top shells and meat, using kitchen shears or a sharp heavy knife. Cut to, but not through, bottom shells. Using fingers, press shell halves of tails apart.	**If a romantic dinner for two is what you have in mind, just halve the recipe. The grilling time will be the same.**
⅓ cup margarine *or* butter **2 tablespoons dry white wine *or* lemon juice** **¼ teaspoon paprika** **¼ teaspoon bottled hot pepper sauce**	● For sauce, in a small saucepan melt margarine or butter. Stir in wine or lemon juice, paprika, and hot pepper sauce. Brush over lobster meat.	
Grated Parmesan cheese	● Grill lobster tails, meat side up, on an uncovered grill directly over *medium-hot* coals for 7 minutes. Turn lobster and grill for 3 to 13 minutes more or till meat becomes opaque, turning once and brushing occasionally with the sauce. Sprinkle lobster with Parmesan cheese. Pass any remaining sauce with lobster tails. Makes 4 servings.	

Nutrition information per serving: 268 calories, 25 g protein, 2 g carbohydrate, 17 g fat, 84 mg cholesterol, 670 mg sodium, 421 mg potassium.

Adjusting The Heat

Some recipes require hot coals for cooking, and others require slow coals. If you don't have exactly the fire you need, use one of the techniques below to adjust the temperature of the coals.
● When the coals are too hot, raise the grill rack, spread the coals apart, close the air vents halfway, or remove some of the hot briquettes. In a gas or electric grill, adjust the burner to a lower setting.
● When the coals are too cool, tap the ashes off the burning coals with tongs, move the coals closer together, add more briquettes, lower the grill rack, or open the vents to allow more air to circulate. In a gas or electric grill, adjust the burner to a higher setting.

Trout with Gazpacho Sauce

4 **8- to 10-ounce fresh *or* frozen pan-dressed rainbow trout *or* coho salmon**
1 **7½-ounce can tomatoes, cut up**
½ **cup chopped cucumber**
¼ **cup chopped green pepper**
2 **tablespoons chopped onion**
1 **tablespoon vinegar**
⅛ **teaspoon dried basil, crushed**
  Several dashes bottled hot pepper sauce

● Thaw fish, if frozen. For sauce, in a saucepan combine *undrained* tomatoes, chopped cucumber, chopped green pepper, chopped onion, vinegar, dried basil, and bottled hot pepper sauce. Bring mixture to boiling. Reduce heat. Simmer, uncovered, for 5 minutes, stirring occasionally. Remove from heat; set aside. Rinse fish and pat dry with paper towels.

3 **tablespoons cooking oil**
1 **clove garlic, minced**
¼ **teaspoon salt**
  Cooking oil

● In a small bowl combine the 3 tablespoons cooking oil, garlic, and salt. Brush outsides and cavities of fish with the oil mixture. Brush a wire grill basket with cooking oil. Place fish in basket. Grill fish on an uncovered grill directly over *medium-hot* coals for 7 to 11 minutes or till fish flakes easily with a fork, turning once. Transfer to a serving platter and spoon some sauce atop. Pass remaining sauce. Makes 4 servings.

Nutrition information per serving: 276 calories, 24 g protein, 4 g carbohydrate, 18 g fat, 66 mg cholesterol, 274 mg sodium, 581 mg potassium.

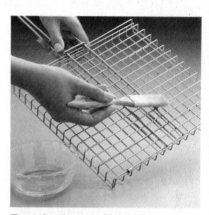

Brush the grill basket with cooking oil to keep the fish from sticking.

After a good day fishing, enjoy this gourmet treat. Just make a sauce of chopped tomatoes, cucumber, green pepper, and onion, then grill your freshly caught trout.

   What do you do if the fish aren't biting? Stop by your local fish market.

Grilling Charts

Refer to the charts on these two pages and on page 78 when you want to know the basic grilling timings for all types of meats and poultry. Remember that meat cuts vary in shape so it's best to check for doneness frequently.

Direct-Grilling Meat

Test for the desired coal temperature (see "Judging the heat of the coals," page 5). Place the meat on the grill rack directly over the preheated coals.

Grill the meat, uncovered, for the time specified in the chart or till done, turning the meat over after half of the cooking time.

Cut	Thickness (Inches)	Coal Temp.	Doneness	Time (Min.)
Beef				
Flank steak	¾	Medium	Medium	12 to 14
Steak (chuck, blade, top round)	1	Medium	Rare	14 to 16
			Medium	18 to 20
			Well-done	22 to 24
	1½	Medium	Rare	19 to 26
			Medium	27 to 32
			Well-done	33 to 38
Steak (top loin, tenderloin, T-bone, porterhouse, sirloin, rib, ribeye)	1	Medium-hot	Rare	8 to 12
			Medium	12 to 15
			Well-done	16 to 20
	1½	Medium-hot	Rare	14 to 18
			Medium	18 to 22
			Well-done	24 to 28
Veal				
Chop	¾	Medium-hot	Well-done	10 to 12
Lamb				
Chop	1	Medium	Rare	10 to 14
			Medium	14 to 16
			Well-done	16 to 20
Pork				
Blade steak	½	Medium-hot	Well-done	10 to 12
Canadian-style bacon	¼	Medium-hot	Heated	3 to 5
Chop	¾	Medium-hot	Well-done	12 to 14
	1¼ to 1½	Medium	Well-done	35 to 45
Ham slice	1	Medium-hot	Heated	20 to 25
Misc.				
Bratwurst, fresh		Medium-hot	Well-done	12 to 14
Cubes (beef, lamb, pork)	1	Medium-hot	Rare	5 to 7
			Medium	6 to 8
			Well-done	8 to 12
Frankfurters		Medium-hot	Heated	3 to 5
Ground-meat patties (beef, lamb, pork)	¾ (4 to a pound)	Medium	Medium	12 to 14
			Well-done	15 to 18

Indirect-Grilling Meat

In a covered grill, arrange *medium* coals around a drip pan (see "Judging the heat of the coals," page 5). Pour 1 inch of water into the drip pan. Test for *medium-low* heat above the pan, unless the chart says otherwise. Insert a meat thermometer into the meat. Place the meat, fat side up, on the grill rack over the drip pan but not over the coals. Lower the grill hood. Grill for the time given or till the thermometer registers the desired temperature. Add more coals and water as necessary.

Cut	Weight (Pounds)	Doneness	Time (Hours)
Beef			
Boneless rolled rump roast	4 to 6	150° to 170°	1¼ to 2½
Boneless sirloin roast	4 to 6	140° rare	1¾ to 2¼
		160° medium	2¼ to 2¾
		170° well-done	2½ to 3
Eye round roast	2 to 3	140° rare	1 to 1½
		160° medium	1½ to 2
		170° well-done	1¾ to 2¼
Rib eye roast	4 to 6	140° rare	1 to 1½
		160° medium	1½ to 2
		170° well-done	2 to 2½
Rib roast	4 to 6	140° rare	2¼ to 2¾
		160° medium	2¾ to 3¼
		170° well-done	3¼ to 3¾
Tenderloin roast			
Half	2 to 3	140° rare	¾ to 1
Whole	4 to 6	140° rare	1¼ to 1½
(test for *medium-hot* heat above the pan)			
Tip roast	3 to 5	140° to 170°	1¼ to 2½
	6 to 8	140° to 170°	2 to 3¼
Top round roast	4 to 6	140° to 170°	1 to 2
Veal			
Boneless rolled breast roast	2½ to 3½	170° well-done	1¾ to 2¼
Boneless rolled shoulder roast	3 to 5	170° well-done	2¼ to 2¾
Loin roast	3 to 5	170° well-done	2¼ to 2¾
Rib roast	3 to 5	170° well-done	2¼ to 2¾

Cut	Weight (Pounds)	Doneness	Time (Hours)
Lamb			
Boneless leg roast	4 to 7	160° medium	2¼ to 2¾
Boneless rolled shoulder roast	2 to 3	160° medium	1¾ to 2¼
Rib crown roast	3 to 4	140° rare	¾ to 1
		160° medium	¾ to 1
		170° well-done	1 to 1¼
Whole leg roast	5 to 7	140° rare	1¾ to 2¼
		160° medium	2¼ to 2½
		170° well-done	2½ to 3
Pork			
Boneless top loin roast			
Single loin	2 to 4	170° well-done	1 to 2¼
Double loin, tied	3 to 5	170° well-done	1½ to 3
Loin back ribs, spareribs, country-style ribs (test for *medium* heat above the pan)	2 to 4	Well-done	1 to 2
Loin blade or sirloin roast	3 to 4	170° well-done	1¾ to 3
Loin center rib roast (backbone loosened)	3 to 5	170° well-done	1½ to 3
Rib crown roast	4 to 6	170° well-done	1¾ to 3
Tenderloin	¾ to 1	170° well-done	½ to ¾
Ham (fully cooked)			
Boneless half	4 to 6	140°	1¼ to 2½
Boneless portion	3 to 4	140°	1½ to 2¼
Smoked picnic	5 to 8	140°	2 to 3

Direct-Grilling Poultry

Remove the skin from the poultry, if desired. Rinse and pat dry with paper towels. If desired, sprinkle with salt and pepper.

Test for desired temperature of the coals, placing your hand where the poultry will be (see "Judging the heat of the coals," page 5). Place poultry on the grill, bone side up, directly over the preheated coals. (For turkey patties, use a grill basket.) Grill, uncovered, for the specified time or till no longer pink. Turn the poultry over after half of the cooking time. During the last 10 minutes, brush often with sauce, if desired.

Note: When testing for doneness, keep in mind that the white meat will cook slightly faster than the dark.

Type of Bird	Weight	Coal Temp.	Time
Broiler-fryer chicken halves	1¼ to 1½ pounds each	medium	40 to 50 minutes
Chicken breast halves, thighs, and drumsticks	2 to 2½ pounds total	medium	35 to 45 minutes
Chicken breasts, skinned and boned	4 to 5 ounces each	medium-hot	15 to 18 minutes
Chicken kabobs (boneless breasts, cut into 2x½-inch strips and threaded loosely onto skewers)	1 pound total	medium-hot	8 to 10 minutes
Cornish game hen halves	½ to ¾ pound each	medium-hot	45 to 50 minutes
Turkey breast tenderloin steaks	4 to 6 ounces	medium	12 to 15 minutes
Turkey drumsticks	½ to 1½ pounds each	medium	¾ to 1¼ hours
Turkey hindquarters	2 to 4 pounds each	medium	1¼ to 1½ hours
Turkey patties (ground raw turkey)	¾ inch thick	medium-hot	15 to 18 minutes
Turkey thigh	1 to 1½ pounds	medium	50 to 60 minutes

Indirect-Grilling Poultry

To grill indirectly: In a covered grill, arrange *medium-hot* coals around a drip pan (see "Judging the heat of the coals," page 5). Test for *medium* heat above the pan. Place poultry on the rack directly over the drip pan but not over coals. Lower grill hood. Grill for the time given. (Grilling a stuffed bird is not recommended.)

To smoke: Soak wood chunks or chips in enough water to cover for at least one hour. Drain chunks or chips. Prepare grill for indirect grilling, adding 1 inch of water to the drip pan and placing drained chunks or chips on top of preheated coals. Grill as for indirect grilling, adding more wood chunks or chips every 15 to 20 minutes and more water to drip pan as necessary.

Type of Bird	Weight	Time (Hours)
Chicken, whole broiler-fryer	2½ to 3 pounds 3½ to 4 pounds 4½ to 5 pounds	¾ to 1 1½ to 1¾ 1¾ to 2
Chicken, whole roasting	5 to 6 pounds	1¾ to 2½
Cornish game hens	1 to 1½ pounds each	¾ to 1
Pheasant	2 to 3 pounds	1 to 1½
Quail	4 to 6 ounces each	about ½
Squab	12 to 14 ounces each	¾ to 1
Turkey (unstuffed)	6 to 8 pounds 8 to 12 pounds 12 to 16 pounds	1¾ to 2¼ 2½ to 3½ 3 to 4
Turkey, boneless, whole	2½ to 3½ pounds 4 to 6 pounds	1¾ to 2¼ 2½ to 3½
Turkey breast, whole	4 to 6 pounds 6 to 8 pounds	1¾ to 2¼ 2½ to 3½

Index

A-E

Apple-Corn-Bread-Stuffed
Chicken, 64
Apricot Ribs, 46
Bacon-Beef Burger Dogs, 31
Bacon-Wrapped Tenderloins, 10
Barbecued Beef Brisket, 61
Barbecued Ribs with Fig Sauce, 40
Barbecue-Sauce Burgers, 24
Basic Barbecue Sauce, 20
Beef
    Bacon-Beef Burger Dogs, 31
    Bacon-Wrapped Tenderloins, 10
    Barbecued Beef Brisket, 61
    Barbecue-Sauce Burgers, 24
    Beef 'n' Beer Kabobs, 69
    Calorie-Trimmed Flank Steak, 11
    Cheese-Sauced Burgers, 25
    Chili-Oriental-Style Flank
        Steak, 7
    Cream-Sauced Steaks, 8
    Herbed Rib Roast with Dijon-
        Sour-Cream Sauce, 60
    Lemon-Curried Chuck Roast, 61
    Mexican-Style Burgers, 33
    Mushroom-Horseradish-Stuffed
        Steaks, 7
    Onion- and Spinach-Stuffed
        Steaks, 6
    Oriental Beef Burgers, 34
    Pizza-Style Burgers, 27
    Ribs in Beer Sauce, 39
    Sonoma Beef Ribs, 43
    Sour Cream Burgers, 29
    Spice-Rubbed Steak, 11
    Stuffed American Burgers, 32

Beef *(continued)*
    Surf and Turf Kabobs, 70
    Tex-Mex Smoked Short Ribs, 45
Bratwursts in Beer, 32
Calorie-Trimmed Flank Steak, 11
Cheese Bread, 54
Cheese-Sauced Burgers, 25
Cheesy Corn, 24
Chili-Oriental-Style Flank Steak, 7
Chinese Smoked Ribs, 38
Citrus Salmon Steaks, 19
Coffee Ribs, 46
Cream-Sauced Steaks, 8
Currant-Glazed Pork Burgers, 28
Curried Barbecued Chicken, 51

F-G

Fiery-Hot Barbecue Sauce, 22
Fish
    Citrus Salmon Steaks, 19
    Fish and Squash on a Skewer, 68
    Garden-Stuffed Fish Steaks, 18
    Salmon Sandwiches, 29
    Swordfish with Rosemary
        Butter, 19
    Trout with Gazpacho Sauce, 75
Five-Spice Smoked Turkey
    Breast, 66
Garden-Stuffed Fish Steaks, 18
Garlic Bread, 14
Grilled Leeks, 62
Grilled Turkey with Peanut
    Dressing, 67

H-O

"Ham" Burgers, 31
Herbed Rib Roast with Dijon-Sour-
    Cream Sauce, 60
Herbed Turkey, 54
Honey-Beer Barbecue Sauce, 21
Honey-Ginger Glazed Ribs, 39
Hot Pear Relish, 36
Italian-Style Chicken Quarters, 55
Jalapeño and Apple Chops, 12

Lamb
    Lamb Burgers, 25
    Lamb Rib Roast with Mint, 63
    Pineapple Lamb Chops, 14
Lemon-Curried Chuck Roast, 61
Lemon Turkey, 52
Lemon Vegetables, 51
Lobster Tails Elegante, 73
Mexican-Style Burgers, 33
Mint Chicken Breasts, 57
Molasses Beans, 28
Mushroom-Horseradish-Stuffed
    Steaks, 7
Mustard Pork Chops, 12
Onion- and Spinach-Stuffed
    Steaks, 6
Orange-Chinese Chops, 15
Orange-Sauced Turkey
    Tenderloin, 57
Orange-Teriyaki Chicken, 49
Oriental Beef Burgers, 34

P

Parmesan Tomato Slices, 6
Peach-Sauced Cornish Hens, 54
Pecan-Stuffed Pork Chops, 16
Peppery Smoked Chicken, 65
Pineapple Lamb Chops, 14
Pizza-Style Burgers, 27
Plum-Good Chicken, 51
Pork
    Apricot Ribs, 46
    Barbecued Ribs with Fig Sauce, 40
    Bratwursts in Beer, 32
    Chinese Smoked Ribs, 38
    Coffee Ribs, 46
    Currant-Glazed Pork Burgers, 28
    "Ham" Burgers, 31
    Honey-Ginger Glazed Ribs, 39
    Jalapeño and Apple Chops, 12
    Mustard Pork Chops, 12
    Orange-Chinese Chops, 15

Pork *(continued)*
    Pecan-Stuffed Pork Chops, 16
    Sausage-Pepper Burgers, 28
    Smoked Rhubarb-Glazed Pork
      Roast, 63
    Spiced Molasses Ribs, 42
    Tangy Spareribs, 43
    Turkey Kabobs, 70
Poultry
    Apple-Corn-Bread-Stuffed
      Chicken, 64
    Curried Barbecued Chicken, 51
    Five-Spice Smoked Turkey
      Breast, 66
    Grilled Turkey with Peanut
      Dressing, 67
    Herbed Turkey, 54
    Italian-Style Chicken Quarters, 55
    Lemon Turkey, 52
    Mint Chicken Breasts, 57
    Orange-Sauced Turkey
      Tenderloin, 57
    Orange-Teriyaki Chicken, 49
    Peach-Sauced Cornish Hens, 54
    Peppery Smoked Chicken, 65
    Plum-Good Chicken, 51
    Saucy Chicken Legs, 52
    Seeded Chicken Breasts, 49
    Turkey Kabobs, 70

Q-S

Quick Corn Relish, 37
Relishes
    Hot Pear Relish, 36
    Quick Corn Relish, 37
    Sambal Condiment, 37
    Sauerkraut Relish, 36
Ribs in Beer Sauce, 39
Roasted Corn on the Cob, 31
Salmon Sandwiches, 29
Sambal Condiment, 37

Sandwiches
    Bacon-Beef Burger Dogs, 31
    Barbecue-Sauce Burgers, 24
    Bratwursts in Beer, 32
    Cheese-Sauced Burgers, 25
    Currant-Glazed Pork Burgers, 28
    "Ham" Burgers, 31
    Lamb Burgers, 25
    Mexican-Style Burgers, 33
    Orange-Sauced Turkey
      Tenderloin, 57
    Oriental Beef Burgers, 34
    Pizza-Style Burgers, 27
    Salmon Sandwiches, 29
    Sausage-Pepper Burgers, 28
    Sour Cream Burgers, 29
    Stuffed American Burgers, 32
Sauces
    Basic Barbecue Sauce, 20
    Fiery-Hot Barbecue Sauce, 22
    Honey-Beer Barbecue Sauce, 21
    Spicy Barbecue Sauce, 23
    Super-Fast Barbecue Sauce, 20
    Tangy Barbecue Sauce, 23
Saucy Chicken Legs, 52
Sauerkraut Relish, 36
Sausage-Pepper Burgers, 28
Seafood
    Lobster Tails Elegante, 73
    Surf and Turf Kabobs, 70
Seeded Chicken Breasts, 49
Sherried Dessert Peaches, 43
Sherried Mushrooms, 64
Side Dishes
    Cheese Bread, 54
    Cheesy Corn, 24
    Garlic Bread, 14
    Grilled Leeks, 62
    Lemon Vegetables, 51
    Molasses Beans, 28
    Parmesan Tomato Slices, 6
    Roasted Corn on the Cob, 31
    Sherried Dessert Peaches, 43
    Sherried Mushrooms, 64
    Zucchini and Carrots, 12

Smoked Rhubarb-Glazed Pork
    Roast, 63
Sonoma Beef Ribs, 43
Sour Cream Burgers, 29
Spiced Molasses Ribs, 42
Spice-Rubbed Steak, 11
Spicy Barbecue Sauce, 23
Stuffed American Burgers, 32
Super-Fast Barbecue Sauce, 20
Surf and Turf Kabobs, 70
Swordfish with Rosemary Butter, 19

T-Z

Tangy Barbecue Sauce, 23
Tangy Spareribs, 43
Tex-Mex Smoked Short Ribs, 45
Trout with Gazpacho Sauce, 75
Turkey Kabobs, 70
Zucchini and Carrots, 12

Tips

Adjusting the Heat, 73
Smokers, 65
Steak Doneness, 6
